MORE THAN A BELIEVER

May this book be
an encouragement as
you relentlessly follow
Jesus!

Love,

Taylor

MORE THAN A BELIEVER

PRACTICAL GUIDE TO A
TRANSFORMED LIFE

TAYLOR EDGE

ISBN: 978-1-79162-768-3

Taylor can be reached at the following places:

✉ taylor.edge14@gmail.com

🐦 @Tedge73

📷 @EdgeGainer

f @TaylorEdge

www www.edgegainer.com

To my wife, Mindy. If it were not for you, there would have been no story to write.

To my sons, Stuart and Austin. I pray that you never wander from your faith. But if you do, please pick this book up and read it.

CONTENTS

ACKNOWLEDGMENTS

First of all, I would like to acknowledge and publicly thank Jesus for saving me from myself. The plans You have for me are so much greater than the plans I concoct myself!

Thank you Mindy for taking a chance on this foul-mouthed freshman. God used you to intercept me, teach me, and encourage me to orient my life around God. Without you, I honestly do not know where I would be.

Thank you mom and dad for shaping the person that I am becoming. Thank you for never letting the differences between each other impact the love you both poured out on me under separate roofs.

Thank you Bruce Parris for sending me daily devotional emails.

Thank you Eddie Nichols for your tireless, frustrating, yet eventually fruitful work trying to convince teenagers that their relationship with Jesus is way more important than the things they *think* are important at 16 years old.

Thank you Rev. John Ryberg for giving me the book The Call and disciplining me.

Thank you Asbury Church for providing fertile ground to grow spiritually and serve.

Thank you Paul Finley for making a campaign promise that greatly impacted my life.

Thank you Tammy Miller for inspiring me to get involved in a praise team and use my gift to serve the Kingdom. I look forward to singing with you in heaven again one day.

Thank you Dylan Haraway, Erin Shockey, & Sierra Jones for allowing me to share my thoughts with you and allowing me to live out my calling. You three are living examples of how young Christian leaders positively influence every environment they occupy from locker rooms, to campuses, to the world!

Jamie Gilbert. Your mentorship & friendship have grown me so much. Thank you for encouraging me to write a book when I had no idea that I could. Your thoughts in the past and the ones you continually share are very meaningful to me.

Thank you Roy Heintz for meeting with me at DD and suggesting that I read Burn Your Goals.

Thank you Kevin Rose for giving me an opportunity to live out my calling when I had no idea what I was doing.

Thank you Dustin Krause for inspiring me to start writing again when I had hit a wall.

Thank you Dustin, Slack, Greg, Sierra, Erin, Jamie, Jeff, & Mindy for reading the draft of this book and giving me your valuable feedback.

Finally, thank you self for be willing to change and making that choice. I am forever grateful that you did.

Chapter 1

SIMILAR BEGINNINGS

All my family was there. I was dressed in a white … dress honestly. Brother Samuels was in the water and after a few words, motioned for me to step into the pool also known as a baptistry. This was June 14, 1981 at College Heights Baptist Church in Gadsden, AL. College Heights was a large church (to me) with a prominent, elevated baptistry. Nice white tile and warm water. It also had the little clear plastic shield about 6 inches high that protected the choir seats from any incidental misting that may come about once a new life was raised from underneath the water.

I am sure you have experienced tile floors somewhere in your life. They are really nice, easy to clean, stand up to wear and tear, tons of positives. But one drawback to tile is when it encounters water, it becomes a Slip & Slide bathed in Joy dishwashing liquid. Or at least the 1970's vintage tile that was used to construct the baptistry at the College Heights Baptist Church did. As I stepped down into the water, I made contact with the Slip & Slide. My foot went up and I went down. What was to be a graceful celebration of a young man professing his belief in Jesus, turned into a summer cookout cannonball off the diving board.

Brother Samuels caught the brunt of the created tidal wave soaking him. Rather than being eased backward into the cleansing holy water, my entry was chest, shoulders, chin, nose, eyes, hair. And remember the little clear plastic mist protector, it was no match for the tsunami as water sloshed significantly over its capabilities and into the choir loft. I kind of doubt it mimicked the scene at the Jordan when John baptized Jesus.

Once I popped out of the water from my premature self-baptism, I was able to make my way to the proper spot and Brother Samuels was able to more properly and as planned, guide me under the water and back up a cleansed young man.

It's hard to see and hear when you are temporarily stunned and embarrassed, but I have to believe there were a few gasps and chuckles that day in church. Maybe God used me to lighten the mood. I think He has been using me to do that ever since. But at any rate, at 8 years old wearing a see-through white dress that went through the rinse cycle twice, I was baptized a Christian. That is a funny (and true) story, but that is not the whole story. It is the beginning of a story that is still being written.

Most Christians have a similar beginning (without the splashes). We are moved to express our faith and publicly declare our belief in Jesus. We are saying that we believe Jesus is who the Bible says He is. That He was the Son of God born of the virgin Mary. That He was crucified, buried, and raised from the dead as a miraculous sign from God that Christ came so our sins would be forgiven. That Jesus came so that we could be reconciled with God and have eternal life. We become a Christian because we believe and want a new life.

That is a vital step in our faith journey. In order to receive the gift of salvation, we must believe in Jesus. Romans 10:9-11 clearly states believing in Jesus is a prerequisite to being saved.

> If you declare with your mouth, "Jesus is Lord," and believe in your heart that God raised him from the dead, you will

be saved. For it is with your heart that you believe and are justified, and it is with your mouth that you profess your faith and are saved.

— ROMANS 10:9-11, NIV

But there is another equally important component of belief. The first component stated above says we believe in who Jesus _WAS_, but the second critical piece is do we believe in who Jesus _IS_. Do we believe that His life is a model for how we should live … today; in the present? And that the Bible is an instruction manual to possessing the fullness and richness of God's love and eternal connection? That He is alive in our lives working for our good? Disciplining us, guiding us, speaking to us; ultimately unfolding His glorious plan for our sakes and His kingdom? That is the complete belief that He is calling us to.

The "first use" of a word in Scripture is often very significant as it establishes the primary or most significant meaning, and this general principle is true in the Spirit's inspired use of 'aman' in Genesis 15:6 where "Abram believed in the Lord" = Hebrew verb 'aman'.

"Then he believed (aman) in the LORD; and He reckoned it to him as righteousness."

— GENESIS 15:6, NIV WITH ANNOTATION

The use of aman in this passage indicates that Abram did not just give mental assent to God's promise (Genesis 15:5), but that he relied on that promise and made a personal commitment. In other words, Abram's faith was not only cognitive (the mental act of acquiring knowledge) but also personal for he believed God's word of promise

"It was by faith that Abraham obeyed when God called him to leave home and go to another land that God would give him as his inheritance. He went without knowing where he was going."

— HEBREWS 11:8, NLT

His faith (belief) was the root of the fruit of obedience, which is a sign that one's faith is genuine saving faith and not just mental assent![1]

But honestly, what I see in our churches, schools, businesses, and families is a lack of this type of belief. The belief I see is a belief that Jesus' death and resurrection was something that God did for us some 2000+ years ago. And by accepting or agreeing with the past, we are forgiven of our sins and will go to heaven upon our earthly death. As long as we agree with Jesus' purpose on earth and we agree that what He did and taught was right, then we've held up our end of the deal and will have eternal life. This type of belief is believing who Jesus was.

With love and without judgement... that is not what God desires. We must believe in who Jesus was AND who He is. A full belief. Aman.

 So, how do I know if I have a full belief. That's a great question.

I used to drive around the country quite a bit for my job. I drove to places like Pompano Beach, FL, Springdale, AR, Arlington Heights, IL, and Charleston, SC. Not only were those places a long way from Madison, AL, but I'd also never been there before. Thank the Lord for Google Maps. Whenever I would drive to new places, I would put the address in Google Maps on my phone. Seemingly instantaneously, a winding blue line would appear on the screen with Madison, AL at one end and my destination at the other. After a glance over the route, I believed it was accurate. So I would turn off my phone and start driving.

Does that sound a little odd to you? If you've ever driven 600 miles away on roads you've never driven on to a place you've never visited, it should sound odd. We may know how to get out of our city or even out of our state, but eventually we would end up lost.

While I believed that the winding blue line would take me to my destination, believing was not enough to get me there. I had to follow its guidance. I had to exit where I was supposed to exit. Turn where I was supposed to turn. If I missed a turn, I had to depend on it to get me back on track. I proved I believed in the route by following it; not just agreeing at the beginning that it was right.

To get to heaven and bring heaven to earth, we can't just look at the winding blue line and agree who Jesus was, we have to prove we believe by following Him. That's called living by faith. That is believing He is.

I feel quite qualified to speak on this subject because I know what it is like to be a believer and not a follower. I lived it.

For the next 20 years following my baptism, any time the topic of being a Christian came up, I included myself in the club. I went to Episcopal Day School from Kindergarten through 3rd grade. I was baptized, twice, at age 8. I was a follower of Christ, right? Let's examine.

In 4th grade, I changed schools. I taught my new classmates 2 bad words. I was the cool bad kid. By high school, I had ramped up my colorful language and it became a part of my social vocabulary. But not around my parents or other adults of course.

Then alcohol was introduced into my repertoire of sin along with girls. Church had not been a part of my life although there were rare times I would go. The longest stint of church attendance was when I was grounded for weeks for doing something bad. I was dating a girl that went to church. So the only way I could see her outside of school was to go to her church. So I went to church…until I was no longer grounded.

There was a man named Eddie Nichols who saw through it all. He would try to get me involved in a youth group, but I didn't want to hear it. I wanted to be around my friends and do the things they were doing, and Jesus wasn't in that circle. (Spoiler alert … Eddie your seed eventually grew.)

Throughout college, my "Christian" life continued. Maybe praying about an injury, using God's name TOTALLY inappropriately, being the life of the party. I was being an influencer not being influenced. I was coaxing other Jesus agreers away from Him, certainly not to Him.

At any point during this time, if you were to point blank ask me if I believed in Jesus, I would emphatically say yes! Are you a Christian? Of course. I knew there was a God and I didn't want to go to hell. I had been baptized. My Christian box was checked. My mouth would say I was a Christian, but my actions said something else. I was as lost as a person could be and had no idea. I was this guy

"But don't just listen to God's word. You must do what is says. Otherwise, you are only fooling yourself."

— JAMES 1:22, NLT

I was fooling myself.

The epidemic that is ravaging our Christian faith is believers in Christ not being followers of Christ.

God's gift to us is eternal life. Salvation despite our sinful nature. It is freely given. All we have to do is accept it. But once we accept the gift, we must open it up, use it, experience it, share its power, and allow it to transform our lives. Stopping at believing will not get us where we want to go nor get us where we need to be. We must use our statement of belief as a springboard into following.

But what does following look like in our current day? The perceived complexity and consequences of that answer paralyzes believers. My aim on the following pages is to break "followership" down biblically and practically in order to free us to become all God created us to be.

PRACTICAL QUESTIONS TO A TRANSFORMED LIFE

- What comes before following? Am I there?

- Why should I follow Christ?

- What traps are there that I need to be able to identify that will interfere with me following Christ?

- Now that I know the Why and what to look out for, How do I practically do it and what character skills and new thought processes does it take?

Chapter 2

BEFORE

"And it is impossible to please God without faith. Anyone who wants to come to him must believe that God exists and that he rewards those who sincerely seek him."

– HEBREWS 11:6, NLT

In my life, there were 2 stages that I went through before I really understood what it meant to be a Christian. Stage 1 centered around my wakeup call and stage 2 involved the tension between the old me and the façade of a new me. Both were necessary seasons for me and may be for you too.

STAGE 1

In May of 2001, it was tense in our house. After delaying starting a family, my wife and I were on month 20 of trying to have a baby. I learned more about the physiological processes of the female body than I ever thought I wanted to know. We tried random, we tried timed. We counted days, we recounted days. She saw specialists, I saw specialists. She took medicine, I needed to be medicated. There were surgical procedures, there were no surgical procedures. She was praying, I was not.

The emotional pain I saw my wife endure during those 14 months was, in a word, angering. This is the woman I loved and she wondered what was wrong with herself. There was absolutely nothing wrong with her. She was beautiful inside and out, hardworking, loving, and all the things a husband could desire in a wife. Yet she felt quite the opposite because she could not become pregnant.

One day after another failed pregnancy test and seeing the depth of the feelings of inadequacy in her face and in her voice, I took matters into my own hands.

I told her that if God wanted us to have a baby, He would make it happen. We were trying to control something that was out of our control. If it was to be, it would be. No more medicines, no more counting days, no more doctor's visits, no more. Au natural from here on out!

Before you admire my righteousness and wonder at my unwavering faith, you need to know something. I often say it doesn't matter what it looks like, it matters what it is. What sounded like a stake in the ground, trusting God moment was quite the opposite.

My wife was in pain. She didn't feel like she was enough. I'm the man. I fix things. So I will fix this. I will shift the blame from her to God. I had a scapegoat. We will put this on God's back. Then when it doesn't happen (notice I said when), we could blame God not her. This was my plan for making my wife reclaim her worth.

That was the shallowest, yet most life changing, moment of my life.

A month later on a Saturday morning, I remember lying in bed as my wife walked out of the bathroom. She had a cautious yet excited look on her face. She had a pregnancy test in her hand. It showed a positive.

I knew there were always 2 tests in those kits. Like any loving husband would do, instead of my first reaction being excited and hopeful, I told her she needed to go take the second one. I was sure her hopes were about to be crushed, and I would have to deal with tears and disappointment at a yet to be experienced low.

Ironically, she had used the other one in the kit in a previous month, so there was not another one. We happen to be going to play golf with my dad that day, so we stopped at a Walmart on the way to the course to buy another testing kit. Unknown to me, she took the second test in a Walmart bathroom!!

When she got in the car, she told me she could not wait and took the test in Walmart and it came back out positive too. I could not believe it. There was no way. We were off the medicine that was supposed to give us the best chance at pregnancy. We didn't plan out, down to the hour, when we would "try". How could this be?

I experienced the power of God that day. He had been waiting on me since June 14th, 1981 to challenge Him. But I thought I had it all figured out. "Fun" lifestyle, beautiful wife, good paying job, travel experiences, nice house. I had not needed God to achieve all this "success" and didn't think I needed Him to start a family. But I challenged Him, He accepted, and in an ironic twist only God can dream up, on Father's Day 2001, He delivered.

Stuart Taylor Edge was born on February 18th the next year.

Many times, before we truly follow Christ, He has to get our attention. God has to intervene in a real way in our life to interrupt us from the "going through the motions" of merely believing.

Sometimes He does that when we purposefully cry out to Him at our own point of desperation and sometimes He waits for the right moment when we least expect it.

The Bible says that God is always near. It is a little hard to comprehend until we see Him work and realize the only way He could have known was if He was indeed near … and in my case, because He was near, He heard me call Him out.

STAGE 2

Once God gets our attention, we do begin to act differently. In my case, I started going to church. (That is a good first step, by the way, whether you are a non-believer, believer, or wanna be follower.) Honestly, I was still a little unsure about this miracle, but I knew I needed to investigate this further. The more I attended church, actually listened to what the pastor said, and actually listened to the words of the praise songs, the more I was being changed. If we desire to truly be a follower of Christ, we have to be open to the places, people, and other voices that He uses to communicate with us.

Some time later after regularly attending church, I truly felt God drawing me in. I had started singing in a praise team, but also still living a lifestyle that didn't feel compatible with this drawing feeling. I am a huge Jimmy Buffett fan and a line from one of his live recordings says there is a thin line between Saturday night and Sunday morning. I felt this tension. An internal struggle between doing what I wanted to do and having "fun" vs changing my ways and more consistently doing it God's way.

Jon Gordon's book, The Energy Bus, he tells a story that speaks to this.

> A man goes to a village to visit a wise man and he says to the wise man, "I feel like there are two dogs inside of me. One dog is the positive, loving, kind, and gentle dog and then I have this angry, mean-spirited, and negative dog and they fight all the time. I don't know which is going to win." The wise man thinks for a moment and he says, "I know which one is going to win. The one that you feed the most, so feed the positive dog."

I believe the same is true of our faith. Saturday night and Sunday morning are fighting. Doing what we want vs doing what God wants. The same principle at work in positivity is the same one at work in spirituality. The one that we feed grows.

One evening I was having this discussion with myself. I remember thinking, God if you will just tell me what to do, I'll do it. If you'll just show me, I'm in. My wife walked in the room eventually and I was sharing this thought out loud to her. She had seen my journey up until this point. She had a front row seat to it all. The good, bad, and ugly. She looked at me and in the kindest, most gentle way you could swing a sledge hammer, she said "You have to seek it. It's not just going to fall in your lap. You have to seek to know Him more". Wisdom straight from the Bible.

"Ask and it will be given to you; seek and you will find; knock and the door will be opened to you. For everyone who asks receives; the one who seeks finds; and to the one who knocks, the door will be opened."

– MATTHEW 7:7, NIV

She was so right (and I still have the knot on my forehead, praise the Lord). I realized I needed to take the next step. This is embarrassing to admit, but I am willing to bet I am not the only one in "believer land" to think this. At that time, I thought the Romans wrote the book of Romans. You can then probably guess then that I also thought the Philippians wrote the book of Philippians. Hey, John wrote John. Matthew wrote Matthew. Why not? I had no idea who wrote Acts. I may have even thought it was the book of Ax at one point which was really confusing.

I didn't know much about God at all. I was not in the Word daily. I had no consistent prayer life. I had no small group. I gave money by guilt. While God had gotten my attention and pointed me in a new direction, I was still an infant. Waiting to be fed by someone else, taken to places I needed to be, not sure of the language to speak, waiting for other people to take care of me. If I wanted to move forward, I needed to learn how to walk… behind Jesus. I guess you would say, to follow Him.

Practical Realities to a Transformed Life

- Whether you acknowledge it or not, God is near. He sees and hears all.

- It's normal to realize you need God but not know very much about Him.

- The game is called "Hide and Go Seek", not "Hide and Then Stand There Until The Hidden Come Out and Find You". If you want to know more about God, you have to seek Him.

- Transformation is a process not an event. Saturday night and Sunday morning are still going to compete for your attention. Choose what you want most over what you want right then.

Chapter 3

WHY

Throughout the bible, it instructs us that living out our faith through our actions (following) is necessary to a fulfilling life on earth and eternity. One thing that I have learned from working with young people over the years is they want to know Why. Not that they spitefully want to disagree or don't trust that the answer given is right, they just want to understand so they can more fully embrace the answer to get the most from it. When I was growing up, the answer to "Why?" was "because I told you so". When it comes to our faith, that answer still applies, but there are far more meaningful answers that compel us to follow Jesus than I told you so. I offer these compelling, transformational reasons to you.

HE IS FAITHFUL

"And so, dear brothers and sisters, I plead with you to give your bodies to God because of all he has done for you."

— ROMANS 12:1A, NLT

The most compelling reason I have to follow Jesus is He stayed with me when I wasn't with Him. While I was dead in my sin, He did not give up on me. When I rejected Him and even made fun of other followers, He stayed with me. He was patient with me. Never punishing, never mad, never pushy. Plenty frustrated, plenty disappointed, plenty hurt. But He patiently waited until I had exhausted my own resources. He not only gave me something I could not achieve on my own in a son, I realized He gave me forgiveness, peace, joy and unconditional love I could not achieve on my own through the Son. I mean, WHO DOES THAT?!

The only person I know is Jesus.

So why do I follow? The first why is because of all he has done for me. To understand the depth of this is to understand the depth of who I really was. Not what I looked like on a baseball field or behind a microphone or a business suit. What lay behind the yes ma'am and no ma'am. I was the good guy that didn't do good things. And even though He saw EVERYTHING, He not only stayed with me but lavished His love upon me. He blessed me with an earthly savior named Mindy who led me to my eternal Savior named Jesus.

> *The most compelling reason I have to follow Jesus is He stayed with me when I wasn't with Him*

There is no other way I would be where I am today without His grace. He has done and continues to do so much for me, even when I still mess up. I am compelled to follow Him. I want more of Him and the world needs more of Him, so I work hard to do what He says and act like He did.

Maybe this was all you needed to be reminded of to start or restart following Jesus. Remembering what He has done for you. If so, please drop me an email so I can celebrate and pray with you.

YOU'LL BE BLESSED

"But if you look carefully into the perfect law that sets you free, and if you do what it says and don't forget what you heard, then God will bless you for doing it."

– JAMES 1:25, NLT

The Bible says in James 1:25, if you do what it says and don't forget what you heard, you'll be blessed. I think I can confidently say that wherever a person is on the spiritual maturity continuum from agnostic to Mother Theresa, they want to be blessed.

When I graduated college and finally got a real job, I bought a brand new Toyota 4 Runner. It was sharp. Hunter green (which was the hot color back then), 4 wheel drive (which I had no need for whatsoever), big tires. And I bought it with my own money from my own job. Man, I was blessed...............Not quite.

Blessed means to pronounce words in a religious rite, to confer or invoke divine favor upon, or to ask God to look favorably on.

In my case, I invoked the power of my paycheck to get something that I would look good in that I did not need or did not serve a specific purpose. Don't get me wrong please. I am not saying you can't have nice cars or cool, good looking stuff. But there was no divine favor unleashed on that Toyota.

But after my decision to follow Jesus, I have been blessed in every meaning of the word. A number of years ago, I had a building for lease. It had been vacant for many months and paying the mortgage on it without any income was starting to get painful. I did what I thought I was supposed to do. I put a sign in front, took pictures and posted on real estate websites. Rarely a nibble from anyone interested. During this time, I started reading a book on prayer called The Circle Maker by Mark Batterson. As we will discuss later, I realized I had wandered off the path again and was trying to do things in my own strength and ability. I was not engaging God in my everyday life.

So one Saturday morning early, I drove to the building. I prayed as I walked a circle around the entire building. I then went inside and prayed in the offices and in the warehouse. I prayed that God would bring someone to this building that would honor Him and the people that worked inside would know Him.

1 month later, I had a tenant ready to sign a 3 year lease. That is what it means in James 1:25 to be blessed by God.

One thing I had to mentally and spiritually come to understand was God wants to bless us. He wants us to have good things, fun experiences, provide for our needs, and fulfill our wholesome desires. He just requires it be done on His terms not ours. That is not too much to ask.

KNOW GOD'S WILL FOR YOU

"Don't copy the behavior and customs of this world, but let God transform you into a new person by changing the way you think. Then you will learn to know God's will for you, which is good and pleasing and perfect."

— ROMANS 12:2, NLT

As some point in a person's life, they will consider the topic of their life's purpose. The question of purpose can come up at any time. Common milestones are a high school senior about the graduate. Another frequent time it may raise itself is graduation from college when the prospects of being responsible for your own life finally hit you. Yet another typical stage of life is the same thing Bob Buford experienced in his life that was documented and discussed in the book Halftime.

Halftime is this point generally in a person's 40's or 50's where they look around at their success and wonder, is this really it? Is this what I am truly supposed to be. Buford describes it this way:

> I have not always paid attention to my life. To be honest, I only began paying close attention when I reached my forties and found myself in a success panic. I was the president and CEO of a tremendously successful cable television company. I was fully engaged in a good and growing marriage. We had a son who was - there's no more appropriate way to say it - a prize.

> And, of course, there was something gnawing at me. How was it that I could be so successful, so fortunate, and yet so frustratingly unfulfilled[2]

I found myself feeling the exact same way. I get calls and text messages from other people expressing a very similar smoldering discontent in their heart that live lives that from the outside is a success story. What we all eventually come to is the fact that achievement, accomplishments, status, job titles, net worth, fancy material things make us "successful" but not spirit-full which I define as full of the things that make our lives complete and meaningful.

For the fortunate, this realization comes in the early to middle stages of life when they are able to change course and find the areas that quenches the thirst for significance over success. For the not so fortunate, this reality reveals itself closer to death where the opportunity to live a rich second half is limited.

Years ago, I owned a business that the world would consider successful. I distinctly remember one fall afternoon sitting at my desk alone in my office with emails to respond to, calls to return, and employees to supervise literally saying to myself "What are you doing?". I was not stressed out because I had lost a sale or couldn't make payroll. The company was in the 3rd quarter of its best year ever. What I was hearing was the buzzer that was signaling my halftime. What am I doing with my life to make a meaningful impact on this world? What is God's purpose for my life?

If you want to answer the question "What is God's will for me?", that is another result of the journey of followership. In Romans 12:2, Paul says by allowing God to transform you (which is what happens when you start to live out your belief), you will learn to know God's will for you. You will learn the answer to the question of purpose.

STORMS COME

"Anyone who listens to my teaching and follows it is wise, like a person who builds a house on solid rock. Though the rain comes in torrents and the floodwaters rise and the winds beat against that house, it won't collapse because it is built on bedrock. But anyone who hears my teaching and doesn't obey it is foolish, like a person who builds a house on sand. When the rains and floods come and the winds beat against that house, it will collapse with a mighty crash."

— MATTHEW 7:24-27, NLT

While there are many promises from God throughout the Bible, there is one that we encounter and experience quite often. We will have trials.

"I have told you all this so that you may have peace in me. Here on earth you will have many trials and sorrows. But take heart, because I have overcome the world."

— JOHN 16:33, NLT

This life is going to be hard. We are going to make mistakes that hurt people. Other people are going to make mistakes that hurt us. A loved one is going to die. We may be called home before our loved ones. Sometimes cheaters are going to win. Sometimes liars are going to get the credit. Sometimes life is just not going to seem fair.

Unfortunately, the devil goes on the prowl looking for an unsuspecting soul to devour. To devour you into a temptation. To ruin your life so you cannot become who even he knows you were created to be.

These types of things happen, but if we are following Christ, listening to His teaching and doing what it says, we won't collapse and be washed away. We will be wise and be able to withstand the trial and struggle and hardship and temptation because we are standing on solid ground. A life built based on those instructions will stand after the wind and floods pass. The wind is going to beat on you and the flood waters will rise. But when they rescind, you will still be standing.

But if you are content to take your free gift, get the free Jesus Loves Me t-shirt, and continue living the life you want, there is a different ending. You get the same benefits of the trials and sorrows. The same vicious wind and rising water, but your foundation will not support you. You will crumble and collapse because you have no foundation. No "go-to" truth. No hope that things are going to be ok. No confidence to say to yourself "It's all good. Jesus said it was going to be like this. If I continue to trust in Him, live out His instructions, I'll survive and then thrive". If you don't follow Jesus, it's hard to know and trust this truth.

Why should we actually <u>do</u> what Jesus modeled and taught us to do? So we can stand. So we can thrive. So we can be sharpened by the trials and stand tall on the other side more prepared and ready for what He has in store for us.

REQUIRE VS DESIRE

"But God demonstrated His own love for us in this: While we were still sinners, Christ died for us."

– ROMANS 5:8, NIV

As we discussed in the beginning, God's requirement is if we believe in our heart and confess with our mouth that He is Lord, we will be saved. We receive His gift of salvation through that process.

I'll be vulnerably honest, this used to be great news. You mean to tell me all I have to do is agree with the pastor that is asking me if I believe Jesus died for my sin and say it out loud in order to have eternal life? That is all that is required of me? As long as I have done that, I can live however I want to (I inaccurately appended that part) and I've punched my ticket to heaven? Sign me up!

That is what I used to think. But now, I want to yell back at God. "That's not enough! We're fake! We don't really mean Jesus is Lord! Maybe Jesus was Lord back in His day, but not now! We just want our get out of jail free card; to collect our $200 and take our place in the room that He is preparing for us. God, make it harder so only the genuine get it."

But even if I did plea with God, He would just say "Nope, have you not read what I inspired Paul to write in Romans?"

> "But God demonstrated His own love for us in this: While we were still sinners, Christ died for us."
>
> – ROMANS 5:8, NIV

He knew that we were shallow sinners and that we would say one thing but do another. He knew as human beings in this fallen world there was absolutely no way we could live out a life that matched the depth of His love for us. We were not capable of equaling Him. So He had to give it to us… by giving and then taking Jesus.

Once you encounter God, you realize the depth and breadth of Jesus dying for your sins and being Lord of your life. What was required, now turns into a desire. A desire to know Him more. A desire to give back. A desire to turn away from those same sins Jesus died to wash away. A desire to live differently. When you begin to follow Jesus, He will start to change your desires.

You realize that the minimum requirement is not enough for you and isn't enough for this world. It may be enough for God by His grace, but He desires us to make a disciple of ourselves and then make disciples of the nations. This is a whole different level of effort and perspective.

In college, I was on the baseball team. My dad and my uncle had both been stars there. I was not quite the caliber athlete they were but because of my name and some ability, the coach invited me to play.

My sophomore year, I remember a conversation with our senior right fielder one day at the end of practice. He said "Edge, if you think you are just going to hang around here and one day they are going to just give you a jersey and you're going to play, you're <expletive> crazy".

I was content being on the team and figured one day even if I never played, I'd be a "baseball player" and be invited back to the alumni baseball games.

Teams don't need people that just want the jersey. They need people who want to play the game. That have the desire to be their best and make their team the best.

God has handed out enough jerseys. He desires 44 year old business men, 39 year old mothers, 16 year old FCA leaders, 21 year old college softball players, 68 year old grandfathers, and 55 year old school administrators to get in the game. And not just get in the game, but play to win.

How do we play to win? Follow Jesus.

PRACTICAL REASONS THAT LEAD TO A TRANSFORMED LIFE

- God is faithful. He will stay with you even when you don't stay with Him.

- You'll be blessed in the deepest sense of the word.

- We all eventually want to know our purpose. Aligning our lives to Christ reveals purpose.

- Adversity and difficulty are a part of life whether we bring it on ourselves or not. We need a firm foundation to stand on to weather the storms of life.

- God has a much greater plan for us than what is required of us. His desires for us is what leads to the fullest life.

Chapter 4

WHAT INTERFERES

"For God has not given us a spirit of fear & timidity, but of power and love and self-discipline."

– 2 TIMOTHY 1:7, NLT

Despite our best intentions to be a good person and to love God and love our neighbors as ourselves, there are forces, internally and externally, working against us. Those forces interfere with our own desire to do what is right and be all that we were created to be. I have come face to face with many of those enemies. They have names like fear, judgement, sin, comparison, & pride. It's important to be aware of them, learn about them, and prepare yourself to fight them. When your intentions are to live a new life, these are the things that will interfere.

FEAR

There was a time in my life when I was afraid of the dark and especially when I was alone. I can remember times when I was at home by myself for the night. I knew eventually I would have to turn off the lights and go upstairs to bed. There was something about turning off the lights and walking up the stairs that scared me to death. I was afraid someone out of that darkness would sneak up behind me while I walked up the stairs and get me. I can remember telling myself as I took each step ... "no one else is here. You were just down there. The doors have been locked all night while you've been up. There is nothing to be afraid of." And I would still whip my head around and look down the stairs just in case I was wrong tonight!

Fear is a strong force. It is a very influential force that interferes with us following Jesus. And there are 2 critical things we need to understand about fear.

Fear exists. I don't like it but the reality of life is fear exists. I used to like reading inspirational quotes about being fearless. But the more I experience in life, I realize being fearless is impossible. The things that cause us to be fearful many times are not real, but the emotion and what it causes us to do are very real. Some things may not scare you but at some point in your life now or in the future, you are going to feel fear. So let's acknowledge it and learn more about it rather than wishing it away or denying it.

Fear is not from God. 2 Timothy 1:7 says that God did not give us a spirit of fear. So if fear exists and that is not an emotion the Holy

> *Fear is not an emotion the Holy Spirit produces*

Spirit produces, it has to come from somewhere. That somewhere must be from the other guy, Satan. I feel it is critical for followers of Christ to fully understand that fear is not of God. So when we are paralyzed and gripped by fear, we are under the control of Satan, not God. Satan does NOT want us to live out our faith. He does not want us to walk in the steps of Jesus. He uses fear to distract, disengage, detour, and derail our journey. Once we acknowledge and understand this fact, it can motivate us to fight it.

WHAT FEAR CAN SOUND LIKE

"And as we live in God, our love grows more perfect. So we will not be afraid on the day of judgment, but we can face him with confidence because we live like Jesus here in this world. Such love has no fear, because perfect love expels all fear. If we are afraid, it is for fear of punishment, and this shows that we have not fully experienced his perfect love. "

–1 JOHN 4:17-18, NLT

The first week of the year, I was writing down my commitments for 2018. "Read daily devotional" was easy to write, "pray for a young person every day" again was easy to write. "Read a book a month". I was on a roll. Then I got to my 4th line. I was very clear in my thinking, but I wouldn't write it down. I thought about rewording it, but still would not write it down. Then I found myself in an internal discussion with myself (beware vulnerable moment ahead).

Me #1 - "Taylor, write it down. For goodness sakes"

Me #2 - "But I don't know if I can do it. If I write it down, I've got to do it."

Me #1 - "But this is something you really want to do. You've been thinking about it for a long time. Are you kidding me?"

Me #2 - "But it's going to take some time and I'm afraid I don't have what it takes?"

Me #1 - "So what if it doesn't work. This is the first step. If you don't write it down and commit to it, you are letting yourself off the hook and even more, you are being the very person you tell other people not to be"

Me #2 - "If I write this down, that means I've got to do it. I don't take commitments lightly. I am not sure I have the time or influence to make it happen."

Me #1 - "Write it down!"

Me #2: - "I know but … but … what if I tell people that is what I am going to do and it doesn't happen? Then they'll think I'm just all talk and all the credibility I've built will be lost because of something I never should have done in the 1st place!"

Me #1 - "But this is what you say your whole life is about. Write it down!"

Me #2 - "This IS what my whole life is about …" <writing it down>

The biggest obstacle in our lives has nothing to do with money, knowledge, skills, influence, status, popularity, talent, upbringing, current circumstances, race, ethnicity, or denomination. It knows no social class or political party. It presents itself equally to the wealthy and the poor. No physical strength can overcome it. Yet we have 100% control overcoming it.

Fear.

A popular quote says Fear has killed more dreams than failure ever will. I totally agree. Fear is an incredibly powerful force that limits lives on every square inch of earth. FDR said it best "The only thing we have to fear is fear itself".

The greatest command (Love the Lord your God with all your heart, soul, mind, and strength) is stated 17 times in the new and old testaments. "Fear not" or "Do not be afraid" is stated 365 times. God knew our biggest obstacle to being all He has called us to be wasn't loving enough ... it was FEARING too much. That is why He constantly reminded us not to be afraid. In fact, the obstacle to love most of the time is ... fear.

God is calling me and you for a purpose. But be aware. Fear will do all it can to keep us from it. And even when we beat it one day, fear will fight us tomorrow. Let me encourage you today to not let your fears keep you from becoming all God made you to be and doing all God made you to do. We have the most powerful force in the universe imprisoned behind a door we have locked with fear. Allow God's key of courage to unlock the door and allow the Holy Spirit to take you to your place of purpose.

COMPARISON

Theodore Roosevelt famously said "Comparison is the thief of joy". I totally agree with that and I would add that comparison is a barrier to following Jesus. Another real and unfortunate reality is when we start to compare ourselves to others, we allow that comparison to keep us from engaging in the activities that can help us grow.

A number of years ago, I was encouraging my dad to join a men's small group. The group met early in the morning which was perfect. My dad knew a couple of the men in the group, and they were all of similar age. The group seemed like a perfect fit for my dad who was recommitting his life spiritual growth.

I made introductions, told him exactly where and when they met, and encouraged him to go for weeks! It seemed he always had an excuse. He was saying he wanted to grow but his actions were sending a different message. One day after another meeting date had gone by, I pressed him on it. I was so frustrated that I had led a very thirsty horse to the perfect cool, flowing stream in his own pasture and he would not drink.

He finally admitted "I don't know the bible like they do. As a matter of fact, I don't know the bible well at all. They are farther along in their faith and what if they ask me a question about it and I don't know the answer?". My dad was comparing himself to others. And it was preventing him from growing

We all are guilty of comparing our knowledge to another. Our looks to another. Our material possessions to others and even our faith to someone else's. And many times when we compare, we give ourselves the short end of the stick. We believe we are not worthy of inclusion. That we are not as good as someone else thus what they have isn't for us. Let me tell you this, YOU ARE ENOUGH. God is ready to meet you exactly where you are and where you are is more than enough for our God! As it relates specifically to you, He is not concerned with what other people have or don't have. He is concerned with giving you what you need.

JUDGEMENT

When we start to compare, what we actually have or don't have isn't truly the issue. The real issue is the fear of judgement from those people we compare ourselves to. "If they find out I don't know the bible, they'll think I'm a bad person." My dad never said that, but I know that is what he was thinking. We resist putting ourselves in situations where we feel we will be judged. Even if we know the situation would be good for us, the possibility of judgement keeps us out.

But here is the funny thing. Who is actually the judge here? We are the ones that start to put together these narratives in our minds without experiencing any judgement at all. Those men had not said that to my dad. They had not been that way towards someone he knew. There was zero evidence that those men would have been judgmental but to protect ourselves, we start to believe in a false future. This fear of judgement so many times is like most fears … False Evidence Appearing Real. We tell ourselves this lie repeatedly until we believe it … without one shred of evidence. I'm not saying there is not judgement in the world, but what I am saying, before you think you are being judged, give yourself the opportunity to be judged. What you will find out most of the time is that you were completely wrong. You created the false evidence.

I am happy to report my dad drummed up the courage to attend that men's group one morning. And not one man gave him a bible entrance exam. Not one man asked him to recite his favorite bible verse. Not one man called on him to flip to chapter 2 of the book of

Ezekiel in under 10 seconds. All those men were there to grow ….
together. And they started at exactly the place where each person
was that day.

There is this another mysterious yet common form of judgement
that becomes a barrier to us living a life of Christian character. It is the
fear of being judged by the friends and groups that we find ourselves
a natural part of like sport teams, our coworkers, members of a
nonprofit organizations, or even a group of social friends. I say it is
mysterious because as followers of Christ, why should we care what
other people think? Especially those that are living lives contrary to
our beliefs? Why isn't what God thinks the only thing that matters to
us? But for some human reason, it does.

This issue is as old as the Bible itself. Even the religious leaders of
the time struggled with human acceptance and praise.

> "Many people did believe in him (referring to Jesus),
> however, including some of the Jewish leaders. But they
> wouldn't admit it for fear that the Pharisees would expel
> them from the synagogue. For they loved human praise
> more than the praise of God."
>
> – JOHN 12:42-43, NLT

I'm no psychologist, but I do know every person has a desire and
was designed to be loved, approved, liked, and a part of something.
We were built for relationship and every relationship has elements of
love, approval, & acceptance built into it. Those things are not wrong,
but where they become unhealthy is when we compromise our
beliefs and character to achieve them.

That is the where the fear of being judged by people in those groups starts to interfere with our faith walk. We want so much to be a part of the group, not rock the boat, not make others feel bad, or even for them to not think we are better than them, we compromise our Christian principles.

Have you ever decided not to give thanks before your meal when you were eating out with friends in a restaurant? What about arguing with yourself about whether you should stand up for a person that is being gossiped about but choosing to stay silent? Ever been in a locker room where the guys are making inappropriate comments about a girl and you join in to be cool? Or girls talking about a guy? Have you ever gone to the party your coworker invited you to even though you knew people had every intention of getting drunk and hooking up?

> *When we choose pride & ego over humility, we get blinded by ourselves & lose track of Jesus.*

That's what the unhealthy desire to be accepted baits you into doing. We want so bad to be a part. To be included and liked. We think "maybe this one time it'll be ok". "This one time want hurt and I'll stay 'in'". Casting Crowns wrote a song called Slow Fade. It speaks to the subtle eroding of our character that occurs when we allow the fear of judgement to pressure us into compromising our principles.

I acknowledge this interference is incredibly difficult to unscramble but it can be done. If you nodded your head to this section, keep reading. There are some practical steps that you can take to help these behaviors.

PRIDE

In his pride the wicked man does not seek him; in all his thoughts there is no room for God.

— PSALM 10:4, NIV

Stacked on top of fear on the wall that stands between us and following Jesus is pride. Pride's slogan is <u>it's all about me</u>! What makes me look good, what makes me feel good, what is in my best interest, and how do I best protect what's mine. A full bottle of pride is what inflates this thing we call ego. Ego's main job is to promote and protect the importance of self.

We have this natural longing to be accepted and approved as was mentioned earlier. Our ego wants validation and recognition. And when we choose pride & ego over humility, which is what following Jesus is all about, we get blinded by ourselves and lose track of Jesus.

> *Who are you really trying to serve with your gifts, you or God?*

One of the gifts I have been blessed with is the ability to sing. I can thank the Lord and my mom for passing down the ear to hear melodies and the voice to make a musical noise pleasing to other's ears. My gift of singing is where I found my door of service in the church. I became a worship leader and served in that capacity for years.

Over the years, the congregation responded well to my singing of praise and worship songs. It was not unusual to have a couple of people come up to me after the service or receive texts when I got in my car telling me how much they enjoyed this song or that song. They heaped the praise on how I sounded or the energy I brought to the service. Even when I would try to fight it and deflect the praise to God, it fed my ego.

Another not so great gift I have been blessed with is seasonal allergies. It seemed like no matter the season, I was allergic to something in the air or on the ground. I would frequently have weeks of nasal congestion and/or runny nose. Anyone who has experienced that knows eventually the gunk runs down your throat and your throat becomes soar. I am sure everyone has had a sore throat. Have you ever listened to yourself talk when you have a sore throat? It doesn't sound that great.

One particular week I was leading worship happened to coincide with one of my allergy blessings. I was aware that I was singing on Sunday so I loaded up on Sudafed and Benadryl. This episode was a little worse than the other times when I had been able to fight the symptoms back with over the counter medicine. A week of self-medicating had not worked very well and Sunday was here.

I vocally limped through our rehearsal praying that God would miraculously heal me or at least remove my horse throat so I could sound good. I let our other vocalists know that I might not be able to sing and they may have to jump in. I saw the deep appreciation in their faces for me letting them know with a whopping 10 minutes notice. When we came out for the beginning of the service, it was no better and there was no more time. The lights came on the stage, the drums and guitars kicked into the song and I was freaked out.

Here is the conversation going through my mind at that moment. "I can't do this. I'm a really good singer. If I start to sing like this, everybody will think I'm terrible. They'll think I can't sing. They will make fun of me. No more "good job" moments or texts. I'll embarrass myself and ruin the song. My reputation as a good singer is done! I'm going to let someone else just pick up the lyrics on the fly". There was a fully involved, 5 alarm PRIDE fire ablaze inside of me. My ego was about to take a serious hit and it didn't feel good.

Right before I was supposed to sing the first words, I felt/heard/sensed a voice say to me "Is this about you or Me? Who are you really trying to serve with your gift, you or Me?". In that moment, I was undone. God had called me on my pride. Was I singing to exalt myself or God? Was I singing for the congregation's approval, recognition, their applause or was I using a God given gift to lead people in praise of the Giver? Was I going to protect my ego and reputation or was I going to serve God no matter the cost? I had come face to face with a conviction of the Holy Spirit and had 3 seconds to decide. Me or Him?

I died to self and chose Him. And it sounded TERRIBLE! I hit about three fourths of the first note and didn't check up. I made it through some of the low notes, but the high notes just didn't come out. It sounded like a pre-pubescent cell phone conversation in the mountains of rural Alabama. "Be_old _e comes, idling on the clouds, _hining like the sun, at the trumpets _ _ _ _ all_. " My voice ended up giving out before the end of the song and all that would come out were faint hisses. Thankfully for the congregation, our other vocalists quickly answered the bell and we finished the service.

I did have a couple of people come up to me after the service and received a few texts. The content of those conversations were more along the lines of "are you ok? It sounded like you were really struggling". But that was ok. Because I learned a valuable lesson about pride that I will never forget and constantly reminds me when I feel the ego balloon starting to expand.

If you are going to choose to follow Jesus and not just agree with Him, you have to answer the question He poses … "Is it going to be you or Me?".

That was my pride moment. Yours will probably look different. There is a great chance it is going to involve Facebook, Instagram or Twitter too. Those social media outlets are a breeding ground of pride and ego. Look at me, look how great my life is, my kids are, look how great I look, look where I am, look at what I'm doing, at what I've got! And please tell me how cool I am and how much you approve of me by liking my post. And it would be even better if you'll comment on it and I prefer things like "girl you look so good!" "ILYSM heart heart" "You're Perfect" and my favorite "Why can't I be you! Ugghh".

If you want to have a really hard time following Jesus, post at least 1 selfie a day and crave over 200 likes with comments sprinkled in. That is also a red flag that signals that you have a pride issue.

Please don't hear what I'm not saying. People are beautiful and blessed and super talented and extra special. There is nothing wrong with social media. I actually like it and think it is a great way to spread truth and positivity. But when it is used to promote self and all but begs for other people's approval for you to feel like a somebody, it's dangerous and destructive. It promotes pride. Pride & ego are the enemy of a follower of Christ. And that leads us to the divine alternative to pride… humility.

Humility

"When pride comes, then comes disgrace, but with humility comes wisdom."

— PROVERBS 11:2, NIV

If pride is the red flag signaling coming disgrace, humility is the white flag that tells Jesus you surrender. Humility is a defining characteristic of someone who is following Jesus. Humility comes when you die to self and resist pride. It sets in when you decide to put the interests of others before yourself. When you take on the role of a servant rather than the served.

The Bible gives us plenty of instruction on humility and being humble.

Humble yourselves before the Lord, and he will lift you up.

— JAMES 4:10, NIV

In the same way, you who are younger, submit yourselves to your elders. All of you, clothe yourselves with humility toward one another, because, "God opposes the proud but shows favor to the humble."

— 1 PETER 5:5, NIV

For those who exalt themselves will be humbled, and those who humble themselves will be exalted."

— LUKE 14:11, NIV

What does humility practically look like? In our everyday life, how do we strengthen our humility and dismantle our pride? We practice it.

Humble people...

- Don't mind being the last in line

- Don't mind *not* being in the picture

- Don't comment "photocred" on someone else's Instagram post

- Don't mind picking up trash

- Are happy to sacrifice bunt

- Typically just lay it up versus dunk it in warm ups

- Celebrates when their teammate has a career night

- Say "We" a lot more than "Me"

- Rarely have the need to be right

- Say "Thank You" ... A LOT

- Say "I'm Sorry" ... A LOT

- Aren't jealous

- Take responsibility

- Don't blame

- Rarely complain

- Forgive

- Serve

The common denominator to almost every humble person you encounter is this one thing. They know who they are. They don't need validation or credit or recognition or approval from others. They are secure in their identity and their identity is not in what they do. It is in who they are.

FALSE HUMILITY

A word of caution as it relates to humility. The humility pendulum can swing too far and humility becomes self-deprecating. C.S. Lewis explains it very plainly like this "Humility is not thinking less of yourself, just thinking of yourself less."

If you start having thoughts like "I deserve to be last" or "They're just better than me", you've crossed the line. Humility is a position of strength, not weakness; Honor not disgrace. To get out of that funk, take the focus off of yourself, and put it back on others. Humility is always outward focused, not inward focused.

SIN

The primary interference, distraction, smoke screen, and trap when trying to follow Jesus is sin. I am sure this word is not new to you. But just because you have heard it doesn't mean you know a lot about it. One of the reasons our spiritual lives get derailed or never get on track in the first place is a lack of understanding about sin.

WHAT IS SIN REALLY?

In short, sin is breaking God's law and general rebellion against God. Sin is what creates the gap between us and God. I have heard it said that sin ultimately derives from our desire to put ourselves above God. You may recognize that now as pride.

You may have heard of the 10 commandments. Those are 10 laws given to Moses from God to give moral and spiritual boundaries to the Jewish people to help them stay away from sin.

When Jesus came on the scene, he set out 2 more commandments that became overarching instructions that point us toward a sinless life. They are recorded in Matthew 22.

"Jesus replied: "'Love the Lord your God with all your heart and with all your soul and with all your mind.' This is the first and greatest commandment. And the second is like it: 'Love your neighbor as yourself.'"

– MATTHEW 22:37-39, NIV

Sin then is living outside of Jesus' commands to love God with all of our heart, soul, and mind and love our neighbor as ourselves.

It is straight forward to understand if we murder, that is a sin. If we do not honor our father and our mother, that's sin. But the sin we can be blind to happens in our hearts. When we are jealous of someone else, that is sin. When we gossip about someone else, that is sin. When we wish someone else would get hurt so we could get their starting spot, that is sin. These are all hidden sin. Hidden sins go against loving God with all of our being and/or not loving our neighbor as ourselves. This type of sin is just as destructive and creates as much of a gap between us and God as "seen" sin.

WHAT CAUSES IT?

Unfortunately, we are all born with it. Satan introduced it into a perfect creation and it's been passed down to us in our spiritual DNA since. We did not pick the short straw or choose it intentionally. It just exists.

Sin comes out of our sinful nature. We were born with this natural bent to be selfish, the capacity to hurt others, to be greedy, to please ourselves. No one taught us this. It's just a part of who we are.

> *Sin will take you farther than you want to go, keep you longer than you want to stay, & cost you more than you want to pay*

The clearest example is a baby. No one taught them to be selfish or greedy. They just come out with "mine!". No one taught them to be disobedient and think they know what is best for their lives despite the fact they only have 2 years of experience on earth. They just come out with "NO!" when mom tells them it's time to go night night. And as we grow older, the desire for pleasure ups the sinful stakes. We have this natural desire to feel pleasure that sin feeds off of. The temporary high from drugs or alcohol, the adrenaline from being in power, the euphoria of winning no matter the cost, or the sensual feelings of intimate sexual contact. Our bodies are implanted with these natural desires that left unchecked, lead us far away from God.

That is another byproduct of a sinful nature. It creates opposition to God and also acts as a veil to His truth. It was my own sinful nature that made me ignore God in my young life. Whenever someone wanted to talk to me about God, I politely opposed His offer of relationship. I've never thought about it this deeply until now but being open to Jesus threatened my sinful nature which I really enjoyed.

2 Corinthians 4:4 speaks to this. "Satan, who is the god of this world, has blinded the minds of those who don't believe. They are unable to see the glorious light of the Good News. They don't understand this message about the glory of Christ, who is the exact likeness of God."

Our sinful nature blinds us to the destruction of sin and deafens our ears to the message that can save us from it. But …

HOW DO WE OVERCOME IT?

One of the most important thoughts from this book and truths from THE BOOK is stated below.

"Jesus looked at them and said, "With man this is impossible, but with God all things are possible."

— MATTHEW 19:26, NIV

We cannot overcome our sinful nature on our own. With man, it is impossible. We are no match for the traps and lies of Satan. But with God, all things, including overcoming our natural selves, are possible.

In order for God to fight for us, He must be within us. Spirit to spirit combat is required. For the Holy Spirit to take up residence within us, it requires a rebirth. This is a beautiful explanation of the rebirth required.

It is through Christ that we are born again. "That which is born of the flesh is flesh, and that which is born of the Spirit is spirit" (John 3:6). When we are born of Adam, we inherit his sin nature; but when we are born again in Christ, we inherit a new nature: "Therefore, if anyone is in Christ, the new creation has come: The old has gone, the new is here!" (2 Corinthians 5:17).

We don't lose our sin nature once we receive Christ. The Bible says that sin remains in us and that a struggle with that old nature will continue as long as we are in this world. Paul bemoaned his own personal struggle in Romans 7:15-25. But we have help in the battle–divine help. The Spirit of God takes up residence in each believer and supplies the power we need to overcome the pull of the sin nature within us. "No one born of God makes a practice of sinning, for God's seed abides in him, and he cannot keep on sinning because he has been born of God" (1 John 3:9)[3]

A rebirth requires surrendering your life to God. A full trust in Jesus. A commitment to <u>follow</u> Him not just <u>agree</u> with Him. Once you do this, the Spirit goes to work; starts the process. Fighting your sinful nature and ultimately changing your desires so you actually become compelled to serve, and love, and have compassion, and put others needs above your own, and become generous with your time, talent, and money.

Deep in your heart, this is probably striking a chord. You are tired of the pain that sin keeps inflicting on you. You think that the pleasure of sin will fill the hole, take away the pain, lead you out of the darkness but what's hard to admit is … it never does. It may provide temporary relief, but the problem is on the backside of that sin comes the same pain and sometimes intensifies it. It is kind of like falling down the stairway of a 10 story building. You fall down a flight and land with a thump. The sin catches you for a minute. Then all the sudden you start falling down the next flight. Then sin catches for another period of time until you start to roll down the next flight. Sin is just a stopover on the way down. Not a pathway back up.

Do you want to get out of this building and start living a victorious life? Pray this with me.

"Lord Jesus, I'm hurt. I'm actually broken to be honest. I have been trying to run this life of mine for too long. I think that I am ok and have a handle on things but I don't. I am tired of running. I now realize that my only hope to be that beautiful child you intended me to be is to turn to you. Jesus, take my life over. I turn away from my sin. Invade my dark places and drive out sin. Restore my body, my mind, my heart. I don't exactly know what this all means, but I want something better. I am going to trust that YOU are the way, the truth, and the life. Not this world. Jesus, I am sorry I have hurt you, but the love of your life is turning back to you. Please take me back."

If you humbly & sincerely prayed that prayer, you repented from your sins. That means you turned away from your sins and turned toward Jesus. You just had a moment of confession which is important to cleansing your mind and heart of your sin.

You have just kicked your prison door down and you are now free. You are a restored child of God and a holy temple of the Holy Spirit. You are forgiven. No sin you have ever committed will be held against you. That is why Jesus died on the cross. To take care of that very thing. There is no condemnation for those that belong to Christ Jesus. That means your guilt is being removed and you are trading your ashes for beauty. You are ready to start a new life of new desires and fulfilling purpose.

PRACTICAL INTERFERENCES TO A TRANSFORMED LIFE

- Fear exists, but it is not an emotion that comes from the Holy Spirit.

- Comparison is the thief of joy. God is not concerned with what other people have or don't have. He is concerned about you in the context of you, not other people.

- Don't allow feelings of judgement to compromise your character. Stand up for what you believe in regardless of what other people think.

- Pride is the preservation of self and our ego. Pride is what makes us selfish. The cure is humility.

- We are born with sin. Without the holy spirit fighting against it, we are doomed to fail. Always remember that sin will take you father than you want to go, keep you longer than you want to stay, and cost you more than you want to pay.

Chapter 5

HOW

Whether you have professed your faith for the first time or awakened to Christ's presence in your life after a period of spiritual hibernation, a very simple but intimidating question soon presents itself... Now what?

I believe that Jesus is who the bible says He is. I accept the gift of salvation. Or I have experienced a miracle that cannot be explained in any other terms other than a move of the Holy Spirit. I feel different. I desire more from my life. I know there is more to this life. But how do I experience it?

I am convinced that following Jesus is the way, but what does that look like on a daily basis? How do I grow in my relationship with Christ? How do I begin the process of following Jesus?

While every person is different, I implemented 4 disciplines in my life that I believe are the key components of the process of actually having and growing a relationship with Jesus. In this chapter, we will explore the role church, mentorship, reading, and prayer plays in our transformation and how applying the character skills of commitment, consistency, & obedience make all the difference.

CHURCH

For me, a critical component to learning how to follow Jesus involved church. I had razor thin surface knowledge of God, at best. And I knew if I want to learn more about a subject, it is wise to go where they taught on that subject. You want to learn math (ok, you need to learn math), you go to school. You want to learn how to play piano, you take piano lessons. Hit a golf ball 300 yards, find a golf instructor. If you want to learn more about God, you go to church. That is where they teach about God.

Through regularly attending church, I started to learn more about God. I learned things that I never knew, learned that there were some questions I had that I will never know and that was ok. I even was corrected on things that I thought were true, that are nowhere to be found in scripture.

> *Don't copy the behavior and customs of this world, but let God transform you into a new person by changing the way you think.*

I once led a team on a mission trip to Honduras to serve with His Hands Mission International (www.hishands.ws) which is a mission that provides water filters that create clean drinking water for remote areas of Honduras. Amazing work they are doing to transform lives in Honduras.

Our team was responsible for helping to make and install water filters in these remote mountain village homes. After each installation, we would take turns praying over filters and the family that received the filter. It was my turn to pray and I was excited and nervous about it. I started out very traditionally thanking God for what he was doing in Honduras and for the family and clean water. Then I started down a road about the children in the home. At some point in the prayer I said "...and as your word says Lord, it takes a village to raise these children ...." and wrapped up a few sentences later with a hearty amen!

As we walked back to the truck, the lead missionary, Joel Aycock, was laughing as was another man on the team.

Let's just say I had gotten a little far over my spiritual skies. I learned 2 things that day. One, "it takes a village" is an African proverb not a biblical one, and two, I still had a lot more to learn. And I knew church is *where* I'd learn.

While attending church is certainly a great start, it's just that, a start.

One day Taylor sat down in his seat at church and as he customarily does, looked around to greet people. He thought he recognized this man but wasn't sure. It's a big church and he doesn't know everybody. He didn't think much more about it and initiated a chat.

"Good morning. I've seen you before but I'm sorry I don't know your name. Do you go here?" asked Taylor.

"I come regularly", the man stated. "the music is really good, the speakers are always excellent, and sometimes they feed us! Hi, my name is Satan."

Astonished, Taylor fumbled, "Do you know who Jesus is?"

"Absolutely!" he said.

"Do you believe he was the Son of God, was crucified, and on the 3rd day of His death, was resurrected?", Taylor asked puzzled.

"Yes, that's the same one. I know that all to be true. I agree with almost everything the music lyrics say and agree with what the pastor says Jesus did"

Really confused at this point, Taylor asks more, "But I don't understand. How can we believe the same things?"

Satan replies, "I guess we both believe the truth"

"But we've got to be different. What ministry here at the church are you involved with?"

Almost insulted, Satan emphatically states, "Oh, I'm not involved in any ministry"

"Well, do you give to the church? Does what you feel and hear make you act differently towards people throughout the week?"

"Uhhh, no" says Satan almost laughing.

Realizing he had been doing all the answering, Satan pauses and asks Taylor, "You said we've got to be different. So, are we?"

Even Satan believes in God.

"You believe that there is one God. Good! Even the demons believe that—and shudder."

— JAMES 2:19, NIV

If we are serious about learning to follow Jesus, we must engage with the church and be a participant not just a spectator.

As a Jesus agreer, I knew I was supposed to go to church, but honestly, I thought it was mainly to show people I was a Christian. Going to church on Sunday was what Christians did. I know to some of you that may seem absolutely ridiculous but that was my main motivation in my early years.

But once I desired a deeper understanding of who God and Jesus was and is, church became different. The sermons started to be knowledge and wisdom not just a 30 minute speech. It was a slow process, I admit, but I could feel a change occurring.

One Sunday, there was an upcoming men's breakfast listed in the bulletin. Up until this point, we were Sunday morning attendees only. No other involvement in anything church related outside of Sunday morning. I remember having thoughts "that must be for the men's group. The men's group are the strong, older Christian men of the church that know the bible and how to pray and help people when they need it. I don't fit into that group. I don't think I should go."

Don't copy the behavior and customs of this world, but let God transform you into a new person by changing the way you think.

– ROMANS 12:2A, NLT

Now that I reflect on it, that was when God was starting to transform me into a new person. Even though I didn't feel comfortable based on where I was in my faith, didn't really know anyone else in the men's group, or really even know where the Fellowship Hall was, I felt compelled to go. Even with all my thoughts telling me why I shouldn't go, I went.

I had a great time. All the men were very friendly and many my age (which was 30 at the time). I got to meet the pastors in a casual social setting. And the speaker had a message for me "How to Be a Christian at Work". A few of my stereotypes were shattered; old men, expert biblers, eloquent prayers. And one was confirmed … a group of men that helped people when they needed it.

They were some of my early spiritual mentors without even knowing it and without even trying. Their friendliness and desire for the same things I was looking for was a model for me. To learn how to follow Jesus, take a step to engage in a church activity or church function outside of Sunday morning.

As I started to become compelled to participate in church outside of a quarterly breakfast, God began to speak to me through sermons about using our gifts. The talents, desires, resources & interests we have been given to impact others. I knew a next step for me was to get more involved. For me, singing was something I could do and was pretty good at. Not growing up in church, singing in the choir did not appeal to me. But our church had started a contemporary band that played at a new style of church service. My wife and I started attending that worship service and I believed that is where I could get plugged in.

But again, the negative thoughts started ... "you may not be good enough for their band, you don't know any of the songs, they have enough singers, how are you, little baby Christian, going to get up there in front of the whole church and be a leader when you are taking your first step off the front porch of merely believing?"

> Don't copy the behavior and customs of this world, but let God transform you into a new person by changing the way you think.
>
> – ROMANS 12:2A NLT

The behavior and custom of this world is to listen to yourself not talk to yourself. And I listened to the lies I was telling myself for a couple of months. But yet again, God was transforming me by giving me renewed thoughts of ... "that is the one thing I am pretty good at, I wonder if they might be looking for more singers, I really want to get involved more here and I need to do this."

So I got up the courage to send an email to one of the ladies that sang in the band. I auditioned, was asked to be in a praise team, and commenced a 12 year journey of growth that started with me singing background vocals on a few songs to becoming a leader of one of the praise bands to eventually being one of the primary worship leaders.

By singing the songs and being a part of a small group that was our band, I learned so much. It also was a huge accountability step for me. If I was going to commit to living like Jesus and lead worship on Sunday mornings, I needed to make sure my life on Tuesday lined up with my lyrics on Sunday!

For the first few years, it was tough holding myself to a new standard. It was a test. And sometimes I passed and sometimes I failed but every day was teaching me more about forgiveness, grace, mercy, power, and joy.

One of the ways I learned to follow Jesus, and that I think is necessary, was getting involved in a ministry area where I used my gifts.

This may be at your local church. It may be with a missionary agency. It may be at your high school or college FCA or Campus Outreach. But wherever it is, apply your gifts to an effort that serves a Christian purpose that involves some level of accountability.

The first answer to the question of how do I learn to follow Jesus: Find, attend, and engage in a local church.

SMALL GROUP/MENTOR

"As iron sharpens iron, one man sharpens another"

— PROVERBS 27:17, NIV

What I have learned more deeply is that we were made for relationship. It's in personal relationships that we grow and mature the most. Ultimately, our sweet spot of living and God's desire is a personal relationship with us.

An intentional personal relationship with a group of men was the second lesson in my course on following Jesus … although I had no idea at the time.

Six years into my decision to reorient my life towards God, things were going well for me. Mindy and I had a second child (without the spiritual drama), I had grown in my faith, I owned my own company, and business was very good. During that time, a new friend of mine, was running for mayor of our city. I helped him with his campaign and we became better friends as we spent time together. We shared a mutual friend who happened to be a pastor at the church I was attending. As election day approached, the pastor asked the candidate to make a campaign promise. He made him promise that if he won, he would meet with the pastor weekly to pray and spend time in scripture. As any good, honest political candidate would do, he made that promise.

My friend won the election and having one appointed position to bring into office with him to help lead the city, he chose me to serve as his executive assistant. So in November of that year, he took office and I came along for the ride. The first week of office, our new mayor fulfilled his first campaign promise and the mayor, the pastor, and I had our first weekly meeting. I did not realize the profound impact those weekly meetings would have on my spiritual growth.

Over the next years, I had someone that was walking me through scriptures. Giving me the context of the familiar verses I was learning in church, enabling me to ask questions, and for the mayor and I to talk through how to apply biblical principles to our lives and leadership. There was trust there, vulnerability there, relationship there. It was a space where the teachings of Jesus started to become personal to me and where I was gaining knowledge and understanding to really grow.

I am absolutely convinced that we need each other in order to learn how to follow Jesus. We need other Christians that are farther down the road than we are to teach us, encourage us, correct us, and prepare us to return the favor to those that will come after us. In my case, it was other Christian men. If you are a female, you will want to find a group of Christian women who can mentor you and teach you. Another thing I am learning is if you are married or in a committed relationship that is moving in that direction, find another Christian couple that can pour into you as a couple.

I was extremely fortunate in that a mentor and small group found me. This doesn't always happen. Often times, you have to go looking for it. You have to be intentional and courageous about finding someone to pour into you that is like minded and that wants to take a journey together. "So how do you find this person(s)" I hear you asking yourself as you read. Here are some suggestions.

CHURCH SMALL GROUP

Church small group. Most churches have gender specific small groups established. Ask your church office or go on the church website and look for groups. I had traditionally thought of Sunday school classes as a group. Churches may also call it communities, small groups, or life groups. Don't get hung up on the name, just look for something that looks like people meeting together.

Admired acquaintance

Chances are, there is someone in a church, in your community, or at work that you look up to. You would like to be like them, be where they are. There is something different about them, a light you might say that emanates from them. You have had thoughts about asking them for coffee, lunch, or just wanting to have a conversation at the ballpark. If this sounds familiar, that is probably your person.

But the funny, crazy thing is you are scared to death to ask them. You are intimidated by them. You automatically think they are too busy. They don't have time for you. They are on a different level than you. The reason I know what you're thinking is that I've had the same thoughts too. My sincere advice to you is take a deep breath, say a little prayer for courage, and send them an email or pop them a text. I bet you thought I was going to say go over there and ask them. If you are where I was, that was just not going to happen … yet anyway. Send them a message saying how much you admire them, are desiring to grow in your faith, and would they be willing to help you grow in some way. There is a great chance, they are going to reply with an "I'd be glad to. Give me a call". Or, they may say they are too committed right now in other areas. Be appreciative of their honesty, and continue your search. God has the right person out there for you. Keep looking and sending messages. Keep being courageous!

Read Books

One of the best mentors I ever had I didn't meet for 6 months. I read his book. I took notes based on the thoughts in that book. I did the exercises he suggested. He influenced me because what he said resonated with me on a deep level. Mentorship does not always have to begin in person but it is most fruitful when it turns into that. But the only way to experience this type of impactful mentorship is if you will quit saying you don't have time to read or don't like to read. You will always have time for what you treat as a priority. And if you want to grow in your relationship with Christ, make time to read.

If you say you don't like to read, it's probably because teachers made you read boring books in school that didn't make sense to you. Don't carry that immature teenage mindset into your maturing opportunity for spiritual growth. If you are someone that needs encouragement in your faith, read anything by Mark Batterson. If you are an athlete or someone that is a high achiever, read Burn Your Goals by Joshua Medcalf & Jamie Gilbert or anything by Jon Gordon. If you need perspective on life, read The Noticer by Andy Andrews.

I was that guy. I hated to read. The only books I ever read was Of Mice and Men and Old Man and the Sea. And the only reason I read those 2 books was the actual books were shorter than the Cliff notes. That is embarrassing to admit now but I want you to know I have been there. And I changed because God wanted to grow me. He wants to grow you too. I am proud that you have started to nix the excuses and have picked up this book! Hopefully this gets you going, and you never stop!

SOCIAL FRIENDS

Begin to have faith discussions with your social friends. This seems obvious but we are hesitant to do it because we are afraid of what they may think. Most of the time, our social friendships are shallow. We don't know what each other is thinking beyond our favorite sports team, work/school situation, or favorite happy hour spot. I think we would truly be amazed if we had the courage to just ask this simple question "How's life?". You'll notice I didn't mention anything about Jesus, or God, or faith, or hell. I believe once we start talking about what is going on deeper in our lives, that will eventually lead to the matters of the heart. And when we agree to have that lunch the next day to have a deeper conversation, it becomes safer to open up about how God may be at work in your life or how they want to tell you how far they've wandered away.

It was in my small group meetings that we tackled topics like identity, sin, and forgiveness which were critical areas of my life that needed unpacking in order for me to continue my journey. One of the best things you can do for yourself is find that person or persons that can walk with you and teach you along the way.

How #2 - find a mentor/small group

DAILY DEVOTIONAL

During the same year I turned College Heights Baptist Church into a holy water park, I also attended vacation bible school that summer. I remember to this day a craft we worked on all week. We created books of the bible out of 4x6 planks of wood. I remember painting each one black and getting black paint all over myself. I remember writing out words like I Kings, II Kings, Genesis, Judges on pieces of paper and gluing them to the "spine" of the planks. And then we glued all of the "books" together in the proper order to make a bible. The point was to learn the books of the bible. It kind of worked because I remember some of the books of the bible and having fun at church, but what I learned many years later, reciting the books of the bible in order isn't near as important as knowing what is in the books of the bible.

When I came to the point of feeling compelled to be more than a Christ agreer, the bible was very intimidating to me. And remember, I had some knowledge. I knew the Romans wrote the book of Romans and Philippians wrote the book of Philippians. (Bless my heart.)

My recollection of scripture consisted of a lot of words that started and ended in "th". Thee, thy, dwelleth, taketh, knoweth. I didn't knoweth any of those words. It also seemed to be written in riddles that I didn't have the secret decoder ring to decipher. So it was not something I was drawn to pick up and read.

But along my seeking journey, I had a man that took me under his wing. He emailed devotionals to me each day. Again, totally transparent, I had no idea what a daily devotional was. But every morning, I got an email from him that had a bible verse (without any words that ended in "th") and a 2-3 paragraph story or explanation of a topic that applied to my life. Month after month, I would get them every morning. Every day I soaked up the bible, a line and story at a time. It was transformational.

There are 3 reasons this made such a huge difference in my new walk with Christ.

Firstly, it spoke my language. I think I had heard about different translations of the bible, but again really did not know what that meant. I thought THE bible was the King James Version (KJV). What I came to learn through these daily devotions was there are different theologically sound translations of the original ancient scrolls. In another a-ha moment, I realized they are called translations because the original scrolls were written in Greek & Hebrew, not English! Again, I know some of this may sound ridiculous, but I want you to know where I was and the crazy things I thought about the bible and scripture that I had never even thought about.

I found translations of the bible called New International Version (NIV), New Living Translation (NLT), and the Message (MSG) that all used words I was familiar with, written in sentences I could understand, and even had introductory paragraphs at the beginning of the books that said when it was written, what was going on at the time, and who wrote it if known. Soon the bible became less intimidating. It became understandable. Here are examples of different translations of the same verse, Romans 12:2.

NEW INTERNATIONAL VERSION (NIV)

Do not conform to the pattern of this world, but be transformed by the renewing of your mind. Then you will be able to test and approve what God's will is--his good, pleasing and perfect will.

NEW LIVING TRANSLATION (NLT)

Don't copy the behavior and customs of this world, but let God transform you into a new person by changing the way you think. Then you will learn to know God's will for you, which is good and pleasing and perfect.

The Message (MSG)

Don't become so well-adjusted to your culture that you fit into it without even thinking. Instead, fix your attention on God. You'll be changed from the inside out. Readily recognize what he wants from you, and quickly respond to it. Unlike the culture around you, always dragging you down to its level of immaturity, God brings the best out of you, develops well-formed maturity in you.

King James Bible (KJV)

And be not conformed to this world: but be ye transformed by the renewing of your mind, that ye may prove what is that good, and acceptable, and perfect, will of God.

If you are having trouble reading and understanding the bible, try a different translation. It could open up a whole new world for you.

The second thing the daily devotions did is put scripture in the context of my life. Up until this point, I was living my life based on a mixture of what the world indicated was acceptable, what my own conscious told me was acceptable, and a sprinkling of truth I was hearing from Sunday morning messages. I could not or chose not to see how what was written in the bible applied to my life as a dad, husband, businessman, coach, son, friend, or overall contributor to society.

Each day I would read a scripture and then a short story written by a person living in the 21st century that explained how the scripture could be lived out or how it manifested itself in today's world.

The bible started to come alive to me. It started to make sense. As the days progressed, I noticed situations where I could apply God's word and instructions. Of course, I had been presented with those same situations in the past, but I never had the eyes of understanding to see it God's way. In a way that would allow me to follow Jesus' example.

While speaking my language and being applicable to my life were very important, consistency is what made the lasting difference. There were 2 components of consistency. One part his, one part mine.

Part One, he sent them every day. He did not miss a day. I couldn't hang my hat on getting an email response from a supplier at work, but I could rely on Bruce's morning email. It had the same subject line and always came from the same email address. Even on days when I know he had stuff going on or was sick, he sent them.

Part Two, I had to read them. Bruce's consistency did me no good if I did not apply my own consistency. It's like your mother cooking a wonderful dinner, all of your favorites, and not eating. It does no good if we don't do our part.

I can remember days when I would get busy and let work or other busyness keep me from reading my daily devotional. I suffered. But I can also remember when I would go weeks and not miss reading it. I felt so much stronger, confident, at peace. The daily devotionals made a significant impact on my life because I consistently received them and consistently read them.

If you don't have a Bruce, let me be that for you. After years of being touched by what Bruce did for me, I started writing a daily devotional of my own and sharing it with people that expressed a desire to put God's word more consistently in their life. So at the end of this book, I have included a 40 day daily devotional to get you started. Do your absolute best to read it every day. I have found first thing in the morning really helps me get the day off right. But maybe lunch time, after work, or even before bed works for you. Whichever the time, be committed to reading it every day. But if you happen to miss a day. Don't stress out! God still loves you! Just pick right up where you left off.

Once you have completed the one at the end of this book, go seek another. There are tons of online, paperback, and even app resources. Check out these links. They are all resources I have used over the years.

Email or Online

Upper Room - https://www.upperroom.org/devotionals

Pastor Max Lucado - https://maxlucado.com/

Fellowship of Christian Athletes - https://www.fca.org/resources/personal-growth

Books

Pious Bob – Written by Bob Pine

Jesus Calling – Written by Sarah Young

Uncommon Life Daily Challenge – Written by Tony Dungy

App

Bible App – Created by Life.Church

Special Note about the Bible App. It is incredible. It has 100's of daily devotional plans that range from 3 days to a year. All types of topics and interests that will speak to you. Lots of well known, wise men and women of God contribute to this free resource. Right now, I am using it as my primary daily resource.

Another phenomenal thing for me is it enables me to carry the bible everywhere I go because I take my phone everywhere I go. And not only is it the bible, it is any version you like. You can read NIV, then switch to NLT, then read KJV, and read a version you may have never heard of. It's awesome. It has been my primary resource for reading, researching, and inspiring me as I write this book.

I promise it will be the most useful and meaningful app on your phone.

SO! How #3 to the question of how do I learn to follow Jesus: Read a Daily Devotional.

PRAYER

Prayer is another important component to learning to follow Jesus. Prayer in its simplest form is just a conversation with God. Using your normal everyday language about your everyday situations. It has been explained to me before as just like talking with a friend. And Jesus is your friend!

But my earliest recollection of what was considered prayer was the Lord's prayer in high school. I learned it and memorized it on a baseball field. Before every game, the team would circle up and recite it aloud together. While that sounds great and on the surface it looked great, I'm not sure it was prayer. It went like this and sounded like the disclaimer at the end of a 30 second radio commercial.

Ourfatherwhoareinhevhallowbeyourname kingdomcome thywilbedon   onearasisinhev   givusdiday   dailybread forgiveourtrespas   weforgivthowhotrepaagainus leadusnantemptation   budeliverevl   thikingdom powrglorrforevernever amen.

I promise it was as hard to understand and say at 100 mph as it was to try to read. That's not prayer. That is seeing how fast your cane say 67 words with your eyes closed.

What it should sound like earnestly is …

Our father, who art in heaven. Hallowed be your name. Thy kingdom come. Thy will be done. On Earth as it is in heaven. Give us this day, our daily bread. Forgive us our trespasses, as we forgive those who trespass against us. Lead us not into temptation, but deliver us from evil. For thine is the kingdom, the power, and glory, for ever and ever. Amen!

Can you feel the difference? Maybe this hits home to your experience.

These are the very words that Jesus taught His disciples to pray but now I realize prayer is a more than memorizing the words and getting them out as fast as you can so you can move on and do something else. Prayer involves meaning, focus, honesty, and it involves listening.

MEANING

I had no clue what I was babbling at an incomprehensible rate of speed in that circle in right field. But now I know that prayer has meaning and my prayer life is a part of the "following" curriculum. Let's take a look at it because I am willing to bet many have had the same experience on a team in their youth.

"Our father, who are in heaven, hallowed be your name" - Right off the bat, we are acknowledging that God deserves respect and we are entering into a holy moment.

"Your kingdom come, your will be done, on earth as it is in heaven" - I had NO understanding the depth of what I was saying here. "Your will be done." That is a statement where we are surrendering our way to God's way. Asking that His plan be the one that unfolds down here on earth rather than our own. That the perfection of heaven somehow happen on earth. This is a significant ask!

"Give us this day, our daily bread" – Daily bread means enough for today. The truth is, our worrisome hearts want our yearly bread or even our lifetime bread … today. Because if God will give me everything I need today for the rest of my life, I can go on my merry way and do my thing. Jesus taught us to pray this to teach us to rely on Him daily. Because He knew if we got it all now, we'd wander off. Guilty as charged!

"Forgive us our trespasses" – Again, he was teaching us to ask forgiveness because He knew we would need it and He knew He would give it. Trespasses (sins) come when we have all we think we need, and begin to trust ourselves again. When we begin to trust ourselves, we do stupid things to try to make our own bread or get more from the wrong people and places. Trespasses. That need forgiven.

"As we forgive those who trespass against us" – We are all going to make mistakes. Towards God and towards each other. We need to pray for God's overwhelming grace and power to enable us to forgive others that wrong us. Forgiving other is critical to our own health. My favorite quote about unforgiveness is this: Unforgiveness is like drinking poison but expecting the other person to die. We think that maintaining our bitterness towards someone and holding onto the hurt somehow gets back at the

> *Unforgiveness is like drinking poison but expecting the other person to die*

other person. That is simply not true. All of the damage that bitterness and hurt does is to us not them. So Jesus wanted us to learn how to forgive others for our own sakes rather than the sake of others.

"Lead us not into temptation" – We might illustrate Jesus' words "Lead us not into temptation" like this: a mother takes her young children grocery shopping with her and comes to the candy aisle. She knows that taking her children down that aisle will only stir up greediness in their hearts and lead to bouts of whining and pouting. In wisdom, she takes another route—whatever she may have needed down the candy aisle will have to wait for another day. In this way the mother averts unpleasantness and spares her children a trial. Praying, "Lead us not into temptation," is like praying, "God, don't take me down the candy aisle today." It's recognizing that we naturally grasp for unprofitable things and that God's wisdom can avert the unpleasantness of our bellyaching."[4]

I may add that to my morning prayers "Lord, don't lead me down the candy aisle today!"

"But deliver us from evil" – There is evil in this world. I think we all can acknowledge that. 1 Peter 5:8 reminds us of this. "Be alert and of sober mind. Your enemy the devil prowls around like a roaring lion looking for someone to devour." It is very appropriate for us to asks Jesus to deliver us from the lion, because he is on the prowl. As we talked about earlier concerning daily bread, we tend to wander off from His protection and provision. That is when that prowling lion likes to bounce. So Lord when we wander off, deliver us (rescue us) from evil's jaws.

When you consider the words line by line rather than millisecond by millisecond, they change. The words of prayer have meaning and they have power.

FOCUS

Earlier, I told the story about a circle prayer I made during my time of need. That was a significant milestone in my walk with Jesus. I was focused, knew exactly what I needed to pray, where I needed to pray and with the humble intent I needed to pray with.

But a lot of the time, I feel like Peter in the garden with Jesus as described in these verses.

> Then Jesus went with them to the olive grove called Gethsemane, and he said, "Sit here while I go over there to pray." He took Peter and Zebedee's two sons, James and John, and he became anguished and distressed. He told them, "My soul is crushed with grief to the point of death. Stay here and keep watch with me."
>
> He went on a little farther and bowed with his face to the ground, praying, "My Father! If it is possible, let this of suffering be taken away from me. Yet I want your will to be done, not mine."
>
> Then he returned to the disciples and found them asleep. He said to Peter, "Couldn't you watch with me even one

hour? Keep watch and pray, so that you will not give in to temptation. For the spirit is willing, but the body is weak!"

— MATTHEW 26: 36 - 41, NLT

When I first tried to implement more prayer in my life, I tried it at the most common time, bedtime. But I should have known better. I am a morning person. If I could go to bed at 7:30 or 8:00 each night, that'd be awesome. Maybe that will be lights out time in heaven.

Normally when my head hits the pillow, I'm on a 3 count. 1-2-3 He's Out! So what I found was I'd get a line or 2 into my prayers and fall asleep. I'd wake up seconds maybe minutes, maybe the next morning disappointed that I fell asleep. Can I not give God 5 minutes before I rest? I was just like Peter!

So I still try to pray before I go to sleep, but my focused time of prayer has become during the day when I am alert but able to quietly consider my needs and praises to God, when I can talk to Him about

If you are going to tell someone you are praying for them, stop what you are doing & PRAY

my struggles and ask His guidance as I try to navigate His will, when I am aware of others needs when they occur and can stop and take a moment to pray for them.

I need to pull off to the side of the road for a minute and address praying for others. With the popularity of using social media to share every waking less than significant life event (not my favorite), it has also allowed each other to connect spiritually which I really do like a lot. Before, I would not have known my high school friend's father was battling cancer. That is a need I can pray for. But what really gets me is when people post a need and their feed lights up with praying hands emoji's or "Prayers!" or "Praying!" comments. If you are going to post a praying reply, please pray it.

I've been guilty of not praying and I think that is what convicts me so much about this. I can remember conversations with others whether in person, email, text, and phone where someone tells me a problem or struggle they are going through. I can remember telling them I would pray for them and as soon as I hung up or left their presence, my own little selfish world takes over.

Telling someone or posting in their comments that you are praying without actually praying is meaningless. It makes them feel better and you look good, but has no heavenly bearing. If you are going to tell someone you are praying for them, stop what you are doing and PRAY. What I do now is before I even reply back to a message where I am going to tell them they are prayed for, I pray first. Then I say it. Because I know me. I get distracted. As we are talking about in this section, we have to be focused when we are praying. Stopping what you are doing gets you focused.

Focus doesn't always mean in a quiet, still moment. I've found I can get focused on prayer while I drive or in a noisy gym. We can connect our heart to God with our eyes open and active in life. As long as we have intentionality in our conversation with God, prayer can occur anywhere.

HONESTY

Prayer is about relationship. But I think we use it more like messages in a bottle. We capture all of our requests on a mental napkin, stuff it in an imaginary bottle and throw it into the air hoping one day it will wash up on the shores of heaven where God will read it and answer it.

For many years, that is exactly how I treated it. If I am honest, in unfocused moments even today, that's how I treat it.

But prayer in its intended form is a conversation with God. An active, in the moment, back and forth, vulnerable discussion of our heart. But sometimes we pray as if we are behind one of those 2 way mirrors ... where we can see God but God can't see us. We think that God only knows the things we discuss. If we don't say it or think it intentionally in our prayer, God doesn't know about it. Think about that for a minute. That's laughable isn't it.

God's heart for us is to bring it ALL to him. The stuff that is tough to say out loud. The situations that hurt too much to even think about. The sin that has damaged our relationships seemingly beyond repair. He sees it. He wants us to get it out. And in prayer is how we do that. Not hiding on the other side of the mirror just sending messages that we think God wants to hear or only the pieces we are willing to share.

But why, you ask, if He knows all things, why do we have to pray it? I've been married for over 20 years. My wife knows I love her. So why do I need to still tell her? What do you know without a shadow of a doubt, but still want/need to be told? That's part of a healthy relationship, we continually communicate for the good of the relationship whether it is assumed to be true or not. God wants us to communicate with Him.

LISTENING

I confess. I am a talker. Anyone that knows me might even say that is a gross understatement. I love to share stories, help others with their problems, and just generally get to know strangers. Most of the time, talking is beneficial in my relationships. But I know I can cross that line.

When that habit of mine transfers over into my prayer life, it starts out good but leaves off an important part of a relationship, the listening.

What if you had a conversation with a friend that went like this?

"Hey, Stuart! What's going on? What have you been up to? You're looking great! Man, I am really bummed about work. Have you ever messed up and didn't know if they would give you another opportunity? Do you think I'm good at what I do? I've got some pain in my left arm. I am little concerned that it may be serious. I am so thankful we are friends. We ought to help that elderly woman down the street. This is all of the stuff on my mind. I've got to run. See you later. Bye."

That is how my prayer life can get sometimes. It's a one way conversation where I tell God all of the things on my mind and take no time for Him to actually respond and help. One way conversations don't lead to very deep relationships.

For prayer to help us learn to follow Jesus, we have to listen. It is in the times of listening where Jesus does a lot of good teaching. Whether that be a confidence we feel about moving forward, a peace we feel about a health concern, or literally a quiet voice in our head giving us a new direction. If we are always doing the talking, we give no time to hear His reply.

It may seem awkward at first, but ask God a question. And then stop and listen. Learn to open up and stay opened up for Him to pour back in. We may not "hear" anything or even feel anything, but I guarantee God speaks. If not in that moment, He will respond.

Not long ago, I was praying for a vision. I really desired God to reveal a picture of my future. So I prayed for God to give me a vision, the vision for my life. I threw it out there and got quiet in my mind. I tried to focus on the back of my eyelids. Looking in the dark for a picture to appear. I focused tight and then went wide trying to see it. Nothing! Blank!

I opened my eyes. I was a little frustrated. Not mad at God, but really wanting Him to move. So I told myself to stay patient and allow it to be in His time. All of the sudden, I closed my eyes again. I don't specifically remember telling myself to try again or make it happen, but I closed my eyes again and I started to use the words "God, what is YOUR vision. What do YOU want it to be"? Again, I went quiet in my mind looking through the blank. Suddenly in that quiet moment, I saw a picture of a place I had been a year ago. It was vivid and clear. I am still trying to discern what that picture really meant, but I guarantee if I had only been focusing on asking the question and not getting quiet to hear/see the answer, I would have missed it.

An important part of developing your prayer life and connecting with Jesus is listening and looking for Him once we lay out our requests.

Prayer is a necessary and important component of learning to follow Jesus. Jesus in fact modeled it many times in the new testament as he would separate to connect with the Father. We must do the same in order to live that deeper life of meaning that following Jesus offers.

Practical step #4 to learning how to follow Jesus is engaging in prayer.

CONSISTENCY

We become what we constantly do. I am sure that is a famous quote from someone, but its more than a quote, it's a fact. 2 books were extremely influential in my growth both spiritual and mental/emotional. The spiritual book that prepared me for a life of following God's call is interesting enough named The Call by Oz Guinness. If you feel like something is going on inside of you but you cannot put your finger on it, go read The Call. The second book is called Burn Your Goals (BYG for short because I will probably reference it a lot!). It was written by Joshua Medcalf and now dear friend Jamie Gilbert. Among many many things, it challenged me and led me to understand that consistency is the key to lasting change.

Consistency is also key to a fulfilling life in Christ. I mentioned earlier about daily devotionals being so important to my growth. Consistency is daily. Not weekly or monthly, or when I have time or when I feel like it. Consistency for me meant every day. When I filled my mind and heart with truth DAILY ... CONSISTENTLY, that is when change occurred.

Think about diets. If you are a "no carb" person, but just eat "no carbs" every other day, it doesn't work! To achieve the effects of a no carb diet, you have to be consistent with your eating habits.

Working out. If you only workout when you have time or when you feel like it and there is no consistency to your workouts, they are not going to produce the desired result.

Trust with teammates, coworkers, family. If you treat people well when things are going well for you and treat them bad when things are not going well for you, your behavior is inconsistent. It is near impossible to build trust with you if how you behave towards them is inconsistent.

To transform your life from a believer to a follower, it takes consistent and intentional actions over time.

COMMITMENT

We can be equipped with all of the knowledge and tools necessary to follow Christ, but if we don't utilize that knowledge or those tools, the chances of something changing in our lives is slim. I like to call that The Gap. John Maxwell, Jon Gordon and other influential leaders have said the greatest gap in the world is the gap between what we know and what we do. The distance between being a believer in Jesus and a follower of His is directly proportional to the gap between what we know is the most wise and beneficial thing to do and what we are actually doing. In order to close that gap and become the follower that we want to be takes commitment.

Commitment involves solemn promises, sacrifice, grit, and accountability. Following Jesus has to be something you finally decide that you are going to take seriously. Commitment typically kicks into high gear when the pain of staying the same becomes too great. In late 2014, I read this.

"I told her, "Burn your wish list. I want to see your commitment list. I want to know what you are committed to doing with your 24 hours a day to close the gap between where you are and where you want to

be. What are you willing to sacrifice inside your 86,400 seconds every day to become the person you want to be?!"[5]

What this passage illuminated for me was it didn't matter that I knew there was more for me, that I felt something different, that there was a gap between my former life and my new life, that I was unmistakably being called to a higher, more fulfilling standard. It was not enough that I *wanted* to be different. It was going to take a list of specific actions, commitments, to be different.

So on November 16th, 2014, I decided to make a commitment list. Things I was committed to doing that day to become the person God was calling me to be. So I opened up the notes app on my phone and I typed out the following:

• Today I will give my very best to God in worship. I will not let my apprehension of raising my hands stop me from giving glory to God this morning.

• Today I will have a great attitude when we go to lunch. No matter where the kids pick, I'll smile and be totally engaged with them.

• Today I will treat Jeremy with compassion and kindness. I will not compromise my principles, but I will treat him with love and respect

• Today I will do this regardless of what happens to me bc I know it is all for my benefit and an opportunity to grow and learn. This is the scary part but i can do it.

That was a significant mile marker on my journey. The day I quit talking about it and started being about it.

See, following Christ is not a religious activity. It is the way you live your life, 24x7. The way you treat people, the way you treat yourself, the way you look at other people, how you serve them, love them, discipline them, correct them, and offer grace to them. It's the words you use, it's the friends you are around, it's the amount of passion and excellence you give towards your work. Following Jesus is not "Today I will go to church". "Today I will pray". "Today I will read a daily devotion". Those are all practices that you adopt to help become a new person, but *following* involves how we live our lives every minute of the day.

I knew I had to start taking specific steps every day to change, to grow, to become better. And my way of committing was to write it down. That occurred every day for the next 3 weeks. Most days I executed pretty well. Writing it down really helped, but there were some of the more challenging days that I came up short. It was too easy for me to rationalize or give up when some of my commitments seemed too hard that day. I knew I was missing accountability.

> *Following Christ is not a religious activity. It is the way you live your life, 24x7*

What was a way that I could let other people know what I was committed to that day so if they saw me not acting or being that particular commitment, they could call me on it? Honestly, just knowing other people would know the type of person I was trying to be that day (whether they decided to confront me about it or not) would be the push I needed to make me take on the challenges. I deeply wanted to be an example, I wanted to be influential, so I knew I needed to find a method of accountability.

So on December 3rd, 2014, I starting posting my daily commitments on twitter (@Tedge73) with a hashtag #TodayIWill. December 3rd's posts looked like this.

Taylor Edge
@TEdge73

#TodayIWill make an intentional effort to smile & spread God's love with those I come in contact regardless of how they treat me.

7:48 AM - 3 Dec 2014

Every day since, I have made a daily commitment to myself. I've now added it to Facebook (@TaylorEdge) and Instagram (@Edgegainer) and started adding other's quotes and thoughts to supplement my own thoughts. Over that year and totally unintentionally, I got some very positive feedback from athletes, friends, & total strangers. They said it was inspiring to read. I started to realize this was not just about me. What was helping me become a better person was starting to positively affect others. So in November of 2015, I started a text message service that would deliver the same daily commitments I was making to myself on social media directly to other people's phones. I realized that we get too busy or even too discouraged sometimes to look at social media but if the little red circle pops up on our messages app, we will always read that. So I self-funded that initiative to start inspiring other people by the same means I began to inspire myself.

I've learned a lot about spiritual commitment during this process. When you are committed, you do not take days off. You don't take a vacation from a life following Christ. Remember the trip to Kenya? Every day half way around the world, I would make my commitment and share it. I have not looked, but the day I flew back from Kenya may have been #TodayIWill not throw up on the person sitting next to me. But I committed to something.

Family vacations on the gulf coast? Every day, I would make my daily commitment. Sick with the flu, down and discouraged by life, mad and feeling underappreciated? I made a commitment. So now, every day thinking about my day and deciding who I want to be today calls on my commitment to keep going. As I write today, my commitment for today is "#TodayIWill be consistent. You don't become who you want to be, you become what you consistently do." So over 4 years later, commitment continues to feed the person I am growing into and becoming.

Commitment is so important because we don't take a vacation from following Christ. When we are upset or disappointed, we don't take that day off from being a follower.

HABITS

What we are ultimately trying to achieve once we are committed and understand the importance of consistency, is new habits. The spiritual disciplines of reading, praying, and church/small group attendance must become habits. You'd be amazed how 40 days of consistent, committed action can change what you do. Just like we can slip into bad habits, we can learn new habits. Everybody can. This is how I learned that habits can change.

My family and I celebrate the Christian period of Lent. Lent is the 40 days leading up to Easter that is designed represent the 40 days that Jesus was tempted in the wilderness. Traditionally, observers of Lent fast from something to acknowledge Jesus' fasting in the desert. This is a time of self-reflection and repentance. It's also an opportunity to develop new habits.

As long as I've been an adult (which some people would question when that actually started), I've drunk coffee. My mom drank coffee and my dad drank coffee. It is something I picked up from my parents. Because I lived primarily with my mother, my coffee drinking ways were shaped by her coffee drinking recipe which was black coffee with a packet of Equal (the artificial sweetener in the blue packet). So for over 15 years, I drank coffee. A LOT of coffee. It would not be unusual for me to drink 5,6,7 cups of coffee a day. And each one had a packet of the blue stuff.

For years, my second savior, Mindy, would strongly encourage me / threaten me to give up artificial sweetener because she thought it was bad for me. While I listened, I never complied. I liked my coffee and I liked it with Equal.

Finally one year, to appease my wife, I decided I would comply with her request. I would give up Equal for 40 days. It was a perfect Lenten sacrifice I thought. I'll give it up for 40 days, she'll be happy, I'll be unhappy, and we'll move on at Easter.

That first morning, it was rough! My morning nectar had turned into a hot bitter mess. I don't think I drank more than 2 cups that day. I questioned why in the world I liked this stuff. But it pepped me up and I got through it. Day after day, I would make my coffee and leave it black. Even though I had given up a silly thing like artificial sweetener, I did it to honor God so I was not going to slip up. I thought I might end up quitting coffee, but I wasn't going to have any Equal.

This continued for weeks. I actually ended up getting used to it. I was disciplined to stay away from the little blue packet and actually started to enjoy the taste of the actual coffee. But I still knew I liked it WAY better with a little of the blue.

Easter morning finally came and Lent was over. "Yes", I thought. I can resume drinking coffee my old fashioned way. I was a good husband by doing what my wife had asked me to do (even if it was for only 40 days) and I was a good Christian because I had not violated my commitment to God. I remember pouring that cup of coffee and spryly tearing the top off of the little blue packet of goodness. Poured it in, gave it a little stir, and lifted it for that first pleasant sip.

It was terrible. It was SO sweet. I couldn't even drink the whole cup. And that was the last cup of coffee I ever drank with sweetener. I still love my coffee but I drink it black. I calculated how much Equal I had ingested over my lifetime. 1 packet has .035 ounces of artificial sweetener. If I averaged a conservative 3 cups a day for 15 years, that totals almost 36 POUNDS of sweetener that has gone in my body.

The point of this story is with commitment and discipline, you can create new habits. If you will commit and be disciplined in reading or praying for 40 days, it will become a habit. It will change you. It will become a part of who you are. That is why I have conveniently provided a 40 day devotional at the end of this book. Based on my own experience, if you'll stick with it for 40 days, following Jesus will become a habit.

OBEDIENCE

Obedience is a very tough word. It involves submitting to someone's authority and doing what they say. If your dad says be home by 10, you'd best be home by 10. That is being obedient to your dad. When you dad tells you to do something, you do it. It is the same for your heavenly father. When He asks or tells you to do something, because you believe and trust that He has your best interest in mind and has a plan He wants to execute with your life, you obey. That is how you show someone you are submitted to their authority, you do what they ask you to do.

In the beginning of 2013, I felt constant stirring inside; a kind of spiritual restlessness. I was 12 years into my reborn faith journey and owned a company at that time. I can remember one Sunday morning in February sitting in church listening to the sermon and just being overcome with emotion. And it wasn't a topic that would typically trigger tears. But there I was, mid sermon, with tears rolling down my cheek like water sloshing out of a baptistry. What in the world was wrong with me! I remember other occurrences in the beginning of that year that would render me in the same state. I decided that I needed some guidance so I went and talked to a friend who was a pastor.

I described to him that I consistently felt like I was walking in a pitch black maze. I had my hands out groping for the way. I was not running abruptly into anything and I felt like I was making progress towards something, but I had no clear sense of what I was doing. I explained the sudden surges of emotion I was experiencing and that I felt spiritually restless. I read a sentence not long ago that says when God wants you to grow, He makes you uncomfortable. I personally know that to be a truth. I was certainly uncomfortable.

After hearing my story and us talking for a while longer, my friend said he thought God was calling me into something. I had heard of "calling" before, but didn't really understand it. So he gave me a book to read that he felt would really help. It was The Call by Oz Guinness, 1 of the 2 books that has made a substantial impact on my life.

> *Obedience starts with surrender, is shepherded by faith & then fulfilled through trust*

I confessed earlier that I wasn't a reader growing up or early adulthood. So when he gave me a book rather than an answer, I was less than excited. I didn't think there was going to be any Cliff notes for this book. I was going to have to read all 304 pages. My restlessness and curiosity was so great, I was willing to try anything to understand so if it was going to take reading a book, I'd give it a shot.

The book really spoke to me. Although it was deep, I waded through it at a slow, but constant pace.

June 21st, 2013, I was driving in Adairsville, GA enroute to Charlotte, NC for business. I could feel the spiritual restlessness come on. In that moment, I felt God speak to me and gave me the words "I want you to make a positive impact on the lives of young people". It was not an audible voice but a statement of thought that was as clear as a voice talking in my ear. I started to cry and had an overwhelming feeling of conviction. From Adairsville, GA to Charlotte, NC that is all I could think about. What does this mean? Did God just speak to me? How do I even do that? How can I do that while I am doing this?

I continued to read my book and ponder those questions. If this is my calling, how do I answer it? I was right in the middle of the best financial year of my company. I was making more money than ever before and the company was experiencing more growth than any of the previous 8 years. How would God want to use my company to make a positive impact on the lives of young people?

I wrestled with that question for another couple of months until one afternoon I was sitting at my desk. The office was quiet and I could feel the sun hot on my back through the window. Typically, I was a go getter. Following up on a quote, checking the status of an order, replying to an inquiry. But that afternoon, I sat there still and quiet and a little hot. Thinking about that moment in Adairsville, GA, my business, the rest of my life. I remember saying to myself loudly although I'm not sure any words came out of my mouth, "What Am I Doing?"; meaning what am I doing here in this office, trying to run a company, and not doing anything to impact a young person's life. In that moment, I experienced the weight of disobedience.

I had unmistakably heard God call my name but I was not stepping up to the plate. Right then, I knew I had to move from disobedience to obedience even though I had no clear idea how or what to do. But I knew it did not involve me sitting in that office. So I decided to sell both of my companies and started hanging out with our local high school football team in the afternoons.

When God wants you to grow, He makes you uncomfortable

It's easy to be obedient when you get a direct order with which you know how to comply. "Clean up your room". But most of the time, God's orders are a little more broad than those of our mothers. We don't know how to comply. We don't know what will happen if we try. What if we mess up? What if we get it wrong? What I found is that I make it way more complicated than it is. God's not asking for a plan. He is asking for our surrender. He'll unfold His plan when we surrender to it. This statement is so true... Man says "Show me and I'll trust you", God says "Trust me and I'll show you".

But the bottom line is conviction compels obedience. Obedience starts with surrender, is shepherded by faith and then fulfilled through trust.

> 'Trust in the Lord with all your heart and lean not on your own understanding; in all your ways submit to him, and he will make your paths straight.'
>
> — PROVERBS 3:5-6, NIV

The line in the sand between a believer in Jesus and a follower of Jesus is obedience. When your tree of belief bears the fruit of obedience, you are following Jesus.

PRACTICAL STEPS TO A TRANSFORMED LIFE

* Attend and engage in a local church

* Find a mentor or small group that you can learn from in order to grow your faith.

* Read a daily devotional. There are plenty of books, online resources, and even apps that you can access on a daily basis.

- Find a translation of the bible that you can understand and identify. NIV, NLT, or MSG are good ones to try.

- Practice prayer. Prayer is a conversation between you and God. Remember that prayer has meaning. Remember to pray at a time where you can stay focused. Always be honest with God in your prayers. Don't do all of the talking. Remember to listen.

- Commitment is what enables us to close the gap between what we know is right and actually doing right. Commitment is staying loyal to what we said long after the mood we said it in has left us.

- Change happens based on the actions we take a consistent basis, not the things we do every now and then. Consistency is the key to lasting change.

- Spiritual disciplines need to become habits. With commitment and consistency, engaging in church, reading a daily devotion, meeting with a mentor/small group, and praying can become habit.

- When God puts conviction in your heart, it compels obedience. Obedience starts with surrender, is shepherded by faith and then fulfilled through trust.

Chapter 6

PERSPECTIVE

As believers being called to something deeper and more impactful, we have to choose & commit to initiate changes in our behavior & routines. Reading a daily devotional, attending and engaging in church, having a prayer life, and finding a group of people that you can learn with and be taught by are all behavioral choices I have found that make a tremendous difference in our faith journey. But what I have realized on this journey is God uses those spiritual practices to actually change the way we think. That is what the Apostle Paul was referring to in his letter to the Romans.

> "Don't copy the behavior and customs of this world, but let God transform you into a new person by changing the way you think."
>
> — ROMANS 12:2A, NLT

The process of transforming from a believer in Jesus to a follower of Jesus occurs when we choose different perspectives. Eternal perspectives. Countercultural perspectives. Jesus' perspective. When you think like Jesus, you follow Jesus. You become a new person.

On my journey through devotions, mentors, church, and prayer, God has revealed to me and I have experienced a number of perspective shifts based on scripture that have transformed me and I believe He wants to use to transform you as well.

Whose Glory Are We Seeking

But seek first His kingdom and His righteousness, and all these things will be given to you as well.

— MATTHEW 6:33, NIV

It's awesome and interesting the skills, talents, desires, personalities, and drive God weaves in us before we are even born. All of those things are made in advance for His purposes but all too often, we take them over to serve our own purposes. And honestly, before I allowed God to reclaim me, I thought those personality characteristics were indeed to serve me and advance my career, wealth, family, and reputation. I did not have a proper perspective.

I would describe myself as a very driven person. I am a risk taker and an achiever. If I put my mind to it, I can make it happen. Those characteristics God intended for His kingdom, I hijacked for many years for my own. Even after the birth of our first son and seeing God do something that even the most driven, self-made man could not achieve, I still tended to trust myself instead of God.

Remember my pride story. The worst praise song ever sung story? That encounter changed my perspective and was incredibly freeing. It taught me a new way to think about using my gifts.

God used that situation for His glory. I had a number of people come up to me and try to console me after that service. I didn't need their encouragement because God had already given that to me, but it was an opportunity to share the real story. My old thinking was being used to degrade me, God's new thinking was used to empower & transform me.

God wants to change the way we think about why we do what we do. For His glory not our own.

FOR YOU NOT TO YOU

> And we know that in all things God works for the good of those who love him, who have been called according to his purpose.
>
> — ROMANS 8:28, NIV

This verse outlines one of the most important shifts in thinking that you can make on your journey as a follower. It is the perspective that for those that love God, everything that occurs in life, in one way or another God is going to work for your good. It may not produce something good right this moment or even in a way that will be evident to us any time soon, but God is orchestrating His plan for our life and is using every difficulty, setback, hurt, accomplishment, promotion, and blessing ultimately for our benefit and to get us where He wants us to be.

It's as simple as being caught in traffic. Rather than thinking the people in front of you are idiots and their sole purpose in life is to make you late, you believe this is exactly where you are supposed to be. Maybe God is slowing you down to prevent you from being in an accident. Have you ever driven by an accident that just occurred and thought to yourself, if I wouldn't have gotten caught by the red light,

I might very well have been in that accident too. Stopping at that red light was working for your good. It wasn't to punish you or frustrate you. It was to protect you.

This example is just a simple shift in your thinking. It is having a trusting calm thought versus a circumstantial emotional thought.

Other traps in our thinking can come from a victim mentality. You always get the bad breaks. Everyone is out to get you. You are constantly saying "Why does this always happen to me?". You portray yourself as constantly being the victim of your circumstance.

Paul is saying in Romans 8:28 that things are not happening To you, they are happening FOR you. You didn't get that job, because you were not ready. That relationship ended because there is someone better for you. Or that relationship ended, because God has someone better for them. Everything that happens in your life God can and will use for a purpose. This way of thinking leads you to heals of Jesus.

When you change your thinking, all the sudden you cannot lose. Everything is inching you 1 step closer to where God wants you to be. Even the seemingly bad things, God is using for a good purpose.

In the book Burn Your Goals (Countercultural title huh? I encourage you to read it.), one of the Romans 8:28 phrases that it taught me that I have used to propel me forward and teach to others is this ....

Anything that happens to me is in my best interest and an opportunity to learn and grow.

I highly recommend embracing this way of thinking if you want to grow closer to Christ. Similar to "things happen FOR me not TO me", this perspective invites us to constantly look for the good. You could be asking yourself "any" and "every" are strong words. Are you saying ANYTHING and EVERYTHING is in my best interest?

I go back to the bible. Romans 8:28 says right out of the shoot… "and we know in ALL things" … not just the fun things. Not just the good things. Not just the things that bring positive publicity to us or make us money. ALL things. Sudden death of a loved one, the cancer diagnosis, loss of a job, torn ACL, stock market crash. God says all things.

I believe Burn Your Goals phrasing helped me the most by giving me the 2nd part. "and an opportunity to learn and grow". Every situation offers us the opportunity to learn and grow. Something good can

> *Anything that happens to me is in my best interest & an opportunity to learn and grow*

be extracted from any situation if we choose to look for it.

My business was doing really well. I decided to serve in city government and let my dad and my brother run the business. This occurred right around the economic downturn of 2008. By late 2010, the business was not doing well and in 2011, I decided to return to the company. Unfortunately with the finances the way they were, I could not afford to pay 3 salaries so someone had to go. I chose my brother over my dad.

That was a very difficult decision for me and created hardship for my brother and his young family. Ironically, the day that I had to lay him off was April 27th, 2011. For anyone living in Alabama during that time, you would remember that date as one of the most deadly and destructive tornado outbreaks in the state's history. My brother and I met for lunch at 12:00 that day and the tornadoes hit at 2:00. I remember thinking a couple of days later that the tumult that was left behind by the tornadoes was the same tumult I felt inside 2 hours before they hit.

So where was the good? It wasn't immediate and there was struggle for a little while longer. But my brother became involved in his wife's family business and became a tremendous asset to their success and gained valuable experience managing people and finances. He grew his skills and experience well beyond what was occurring working for me. So what appeared on the surface as a tragedy, God worked for my brothers good. Me setting him free truly was in his best interest and an opportunity to learn and grow. We also have a stronger relationship now than we ever did working together. In ALL things, God works for the good of those who love Him.

God wants to tell you today that He has a plan. And His ways are not our ways. We may not (and usually do not) understand at the time, but that is why God's word says lean not on your own understanding.

He will transform you if you will allow Him to change the way you think starting with all things are working for your good and offer you an opportunity to learn and grow through His love.

MISSING OUT

"For the kingdom of heaven is like a landowner who went out early in the morning to hire workers for his vineyard. He agreed to pay them a denarius for the day and sent them into his vineyard.

"About nine in the morning he went out and saw others standing in the marketplace doing nothing. So they went. "He went out again about noon and about three in the afternoon and did the same thing. About five in the afternoon he went out and found still others standing around.

He asked them, 'Why have you been standing here all day long doing nothing?' " 'Because no one has hired us,' they answered. "He said to them, 'You also go and work in my vineyard.' "When evening came, the owner of the vineyard said to his foreman, 'Call the workers and pay them their wages, beginning with the last ones hired and going on to the first.' "The workers who were hired about five in the afternoon came and each received a denarius. So when those came who were hired first, they expected to receive more.

But each one of them also received a denarius. When they received it, they began to grumble against the landowner. 'These who were hired last worked only one hour,' they said, 'and you have made them equal to us who have borne the burden of the work and the heat of the day."

– MATTHEW 20:1-12, NIV

As I started to invest my time reading scripture, I remember reading this story, and it being very hard to swallow. My first thoughts were, that's not fair to the first worker. But I had to change my thinking. God changed my perspective by revealing it through a different lens.

My version was the first worker hired was like a little boy who accepted Christ when he was very young and embraced Jesus' teachings and lived a clean life. No wild partying, didn't get drunk on the weekends when he was a teenager, volunteered to help at community events, and was active in his church. He grew in his faith and was as respected a man that existed in the community and to God. We will call him Mr. Right.

And then there was the last worker hired. He was the guy that made fun of the first guy although he called himself a Christian. He loved to be the center of attention, thought of people that went to church as uncool, had his life all planned out, women, alcohol, fast cars, finest restaurants. He would live up the "fun" life. And that was the behavior he embraced until late in life. We'll call him Mr. Fun. All that "fun" led to broken relationships, no respect among his peers or younger people, list of regrets a mile long, and a feeling of emptiness. Mr. Fun finally accepted Christ the day before he died. He got the same abundant wage.

One of those men REALLY missed out. They both got into heaven (thank you Jesus), but they didn't both receive the joy from life. I used to think it was Mr. Right that really missed out but now I know it was Mr. Fun.

Another shift in our mindset is what we think we are giving up if we go all in and follow Christ. A life of a follower is as much fun as a believer but is richer and fulfilling. Followers still buy nice things, have good paying jobs, go on fun trips, live in nice houses, are competitive sports fanatics, and drink wine on the patio on a nice summer evening. Going into a deeper relationship with Christ doesn't mean you give up fun. What becomes fun just changes.

> *Going into a deeper relationship with Christ doesn't mean you give up fun*

Staying out until 1 AM with your friends laughing all night still occurs. Is just occurs without playing beer pong all night, someone getting sick or mad or both and waking up the next morning wondering why in the world they thought that was fun.

It happens having friends over for dinner and enjoying a couple of glasses of wine talking about life and the future. And someone being responsible enough to drink water instead and driving home. Then waking up the next morning looking forward to the next time you can get together.

If you love to travel as I do, you don't have to give up traveling. But instead of the all-inclusive posh island resort every year, maybe it's a mission trip to Kenya. Many times when I've come back from the island trips, I think about the experience but I also think about the money I spent. When I came back from Kenya, I thought about the experience and then about the change I see going on in the world for good. Traveling on mission is fun with a lasting impacting.

To move to the next level in our spiritual lives, we must open our minds to a more fulfilling, lasting way to enjoy ourselves that involves

Christian values, serving others, and honoring God. Living in our old ways is where we are really missing out.

ENOUGH

"The thief comes only to steal and kill and destroy; I have come that they may have life, and have it to the full."

— JOHN 10:10, NIV

Jesus came, died, and rose so we would have a full life as He is quoted as saying in John. But the mindset we have to battle and overcome to live into that fullness, or as some other translations say abundance, is the perception of lack or that we are not enough or we do not have enough.

The idea of lack is one of the biggest chasms that must be traversed in order to move from believer to follower. To experience God's abundance, we must be generous. It is better to give than to receive. That is what the bible tells us and I have experienced. But Satan, the thief, steals, kills, and destroys that belief using the weapon of lack.

MONEY

It comes in our financial giving. We think we cannot give because we do not have enough money. We need our money to take care of ourselves and our family. We think we lack the financial resources to give to the church and those in need. That is a flat out lie.

The truth is we think we can't maintain our current high standard of living if we give. We can't afford the nice dinners, fun vacations, and stylish clothes if we give our money away. Maybe I am the only one that had these thoughts?

I'm just telling you out of my own experience, if you have enough money to buy this book, you have enough to give for God's work and God's people. If you can't give 10%, give 5%. If you can't give 5%, give 2%. If you can't give 1%, give $1. Battle the devil's attacks by overcoming the mindset of lack. You can do that by giving. Every time I have made a choice to think of God's abundance instead of the devil's lack, I have been blessed. You will find that you have more than enough (abundance) when you will battle the mindset of lack of money.

TIME

The devil really goes on the offensive with our time. How many times have you said you do not have enough time? You don't have enough time to read a devotion. You don't have enough time to go on a mission trip. You don't have enough time to go to lunch with a friend that is hurting. You don't have enough time to volunteer at a local nonprofit.

I've heard it said that idle time is the devil's workshop, but I would say that busyness is his more effective tool. We have to rethink how we are spending our time and why we are spending our time. What are we trying to produce with our time. I am afraid if most of us honestly answer that question, we would say mere survival. We would probably not even say trying to get ahead (whatever that means) and say just trying to keep up. When we come up with those answers, the devil has us right where he wants us. Over there on the sidelines of life riding the stationary bike. Spending a whole lot of energy going nowhere and feeling tired and empty.

Every one of us has 86,400 seconds in a day. Jesus, Paul, Peter, Martin Luther King, Nelson Mandela, you and me. We all do not lack time. We all have the same. We just need to change the way we think about how we are using it and what we want it to produce.

Lack

So we know now these "lack" mindsets come from the devil but how does he plant them? A friend of mine stopped me in my tracks one day when he said this … "The devil's favorite voice is our own".

The devil uses our own familiar voice against us. He grabs the microphone and cranks up the volume. It's silent to the world around us but deafening inside our head. Have you told yourself these things before? Have these thoughts scrolled across your mental marquee?

You're not smart enough

You're not pretty enough

You're not strong enough

You're not interesting enough

You're not creative enough

You're not vocal enough

You're not fast enough

You're not tall enough

You're not cool enough

You're not _____ enough

They have crossed mine too. These are the hijacked thoughts and self-talk that create our lack mentality. When the devil has fully planted that lack mentality in your mind, he's got you. Because once you start thinking that way, you start acting that way. It's very difficult to follow Christ where He wants to take you because you "think" you are not enough.

> *The devil's favorite voice is our own*

But here is the nuance of this all. Without Jesus, we are not enough. With Jesus, we are more than enough.

Paul said this to the church at Ephesus, but I can hear his words of truth speaking to us today "I pray that from his glorious, unlimited resources he will empower you with inner strength through his Spirit"

God has UNLIMITED resources. When we decide to follow Jesus, He will empower us through the Holy Spirit to make us more than enough. There is no lack in that.

Are you still not there with the word UNLIMITED? Still wonder if you can be enough even with an unlimited supply of resources? This should then be the knockout punch!

> "Now all glory to God, who is able through His mighty power at work within us, to accomplish infinitely more than we might ask or think".
>
> — EPHESIANS 3:20, NLT

God through His mighty power (not ours) working within us is able to accomplish INFINITELY (that's kin to UNLIMITED) … MORE … than we may ask or THINK! Our thinking! That is what we have been talking about and living with that is creating this false lack mentality.

So whatever you have been thinking you do not have enough of... that's over. Choosing to follow Jesus empowers you with more than enough!

What's Possible

As I have walked under the authority and leadership of Jesus, my perspective of what's truly possible in life has changed as well. But it's probably not what you are thinking.

One of the most famous verses of the Bible is Philippians 4:13. 'I can do all things through Christ who strengthens me.'

I remember seeing this verse written under the eyes of a fierce competitor, national championship quarterback, and Heisman trophy winner at the University of Florida named Tim Tebow. He was and still is a Christian role model for me personally and thousands if not millions of young athletes around the world. When I used to think of doing all things through Christ, I thought of winning ... like Tim Tebow. Tough quarterback sneaks, jump passes, fiery motivational speeches. He could do all of those great things because of Christ's strength. I know now what Tebow really meant with that verse.

With Christ on my side, I can accomplish great, fun, praiseworthy things. I sincerely do think that is true but that is not that verse's true meaning.

'Not that I was ever in need, for I have learned how to be content with whatever I have. I know how to live on almost nothing or with everything. I have learned the secret of living in every situation, whether it is with a full stomach or empty, with plenty or little. '

— PHILIPPIANS 4:11-12, NLT

In 2015, I travelled to Kenya on a mission trip. During this time, an Ebola outbreak had occurred in western Africa and was affecting other parts of the world. Kenya was not one of the countries of concern as it is on the eastern side of the continent so I travelled there feeling very safe.

The day I was flying home, I did not feel well. So I flew 11 hours from Nairobi, Kenya to Amsterdam, Netherlands sick at my stomach. To make matters worse, I then flew another 9 hours from Amsterdam to Atlanta with this same sick feeling. It was everything I could mentally and spiritually do to keep from vomiting or you know … the other end. It was a miserable feeling but I made it.

When I got home, I still continued to feel sick and became sick. After a few days, I could not wait it out so I went to the local urgent care to find relief. My symptoms were the typical stomach virus type of symptoms. I figured I would get a shot or steroid and be on my way. Not exactly.

Once my name was called, the nurse technician took me into the small holding pen I call it with the curtain. Weight, blood pressure, heart rate, "what brought you in today", the normal stuff. I described my symptoms and how long I had felt this way. The nice young girl recorded it all as normal. As we walked into the examining room where the doctor was to see me, I mentioned that I had just gotten back from Africa on a mission trip and was happy that I did not get sick until the last day. We exchanged smiles and she said the doctor would be in shortly.

Note to any of you future doctors out there. The walls and doors of an urgent care office are not that thick. Patients can hear about everything you are saying out there. General life note ... just because a person cannot see you doesn't mean they cannot hear you. Back to the story.

A few minutes later I clearly heard a male voice outside the room agitatedly exclaim, "WHY DID HE COME HERE!" and then a lot of commotion. The next words I could understand were "Call the CDC". Moments later, the sweet young nurse technician walked through the door wearing a surgical mask and handed me one. With almost tears in her eyes she said, "I am so sorry about this, but we need you to put this on. The doctor is checking on some things and will be in in a minute".

Right then it hit me. I had been seeing on the news the protocol hospitals had been employing when they encountered an Ebola patient. Masks. Minimal contact. Quarantine. CDC reporting. They thought Ebola had just come to Madison, AL and his name was Taylor Edge.

I could tell the young lady was scared. She was the only person that had contact with me. Their protocol was to isolate the infected and anyone who had come into contact with the infected. In her mind, she was now part of the problem.

Philippians 4:12 says "I have learned the secret to living in every situation....". THEN Philippians 4:13 tells us the secret. I can do ALL THINGS through Christ who gives me strength. I can all of the sudden be calm and encouraging to a young medical technician who thinks her life just changed forever because Christ gives me the strength to do it. I can stay calm in a waiting room while a doctor calls the Center for Disease Control to figure out what to do with an Ebola patient through Christ that strengthens me. I can pray with conviction that God has a plan for this situation and I can trust Him with my sick life through Christ who strengthens me.

Philippians 4:13 means no matter your circumstances whether mountain high or valley low, you can persevere, endure, trust, have hope because of the strength that a relationship with Jesus provides. Everything you do is empowered by Christ. Every job promotion and every layoff. Every home run and every strike out. Every lapse of sinful desire and every faithful spiritual victory.

About 10 minutes passed and a doctor walked in in the room … without a mask. He explained that he called the CDC and based on the country I visited and my specific symptoms, I did not have Ebola. I had something bad, but it was treatable. But there was a 20 minute stretch there where I knew what it meant to be full and I knew then what it felt like to be empty. But through it all my relationship with Jesus enabled me to do those things.

Matthew 19:26 Jesus said "…with man, this is impossible. But with God, all things are possible"

No matter your situation, circumstance, past mistakes, where you came from, or where it looks like you are going, all things are possible through Christ who strengthens you! Allow God to transform the way you think about what is possible.

IDENTITY

Another important perspective shift that God makes in our spiritual maturation process is where we derive our value. Have you ever been asked the question "Who are you?". Maybe you have asked that to the person in the mirror.

The way you answer that question reveals where you derive you value. As we discussed in chapter 4, pride can really distort that answer. Because we have a desire to be successful and "somebody", we extract our value as a person many times from what we do. The more prestigious our job or cooler the team we play for, the more value we feel. Then, as a double shot, the more recognition and attention we receive from what we do, we assign ourselves even more value. So you hear things like this…

"I'm a New York Times bestselling author."

"I'm an All SEC defensive back"

"I'm the owner of a multimillion dollar company"

Do you hear the value assignment. Not only is their value as being an author, a football player, or a business owner, but they have

> *Our value as a person & who we are is rooted in whose we are*

assigned even more value to themselves because of the recognition and status they've achieved. I'm not diminishing the hard work, sacrifice, gifts, and skills it took to become those labels, but that's what they do, not who they are.

And the problem with tying our value to what we do is the fact that those things can be taken away. People can stop buying your book because a better book comes along. You can tear an ACL and no longer play football. A recession can hit and businesses close. If we are only somebody with those things, we are nobody without them? You were a football player, but because of injury, you now are not. You are still living and breathing and exist, so who are you?

That's a tough question to face if we assign our value to what we do and it is taken away.

As we begin to be transformed by Christ, we have a different answer to that question. We start to realize our value as a person and who we are is rooted in *whose* we are. I go back to the realization that Jesus pursued me when I did not want anything to do with him. I didn't need Him. I was willingly and arrogantly living a life seeking the approval of the world not Him. AND EVEN. THEN. He rescued me. He didn't care how much money I had, where I had travelled in the world, or how many high profile friends I had… or how many sins I had committed. He saw the true value that had been covered up by all of the worldly stuff. And He patiently fought to take hold of me until I was ready. That my friends lets you know your true value!

So now I and other followers of Christ are secure in who we are. We are children of God and are inheriting His qualities. Our answer to who am I should then describe our character not our activity. When we are awakened to the reality of who we are in Christ, we start to understand that we have gifts and talents and skills and callings. God made us a specific way and that is who we are. And from that, we are then commissioned by Him to go do things.

I was one of those 3 "titles" I mentioned a few pages back (and if you've seen me, you've ruled out the All SEC defensive back). But I have learned that my value was not based on the fact that I was the title. My value is in how God made me. The gifts, desires, skills, and personality that He gave me. And He has a purpose for those gifts. But because of pride, we hijack them for our own glory.

When we truly surrender to Jesus, He starts to open our eyes to the words that describe our value. It takes time, attention, and intention on our part. But as we start to follow based on the simple ways I outlined in this book, He will reveal it to us. So when someone asks me who I am now, I don't say former business owner. I say I am an encourager. I am an energy giver. I am an optimist. I am a problem solver. I am a follower of Christ. That is who I am.

And *then* I do not mind answering the question "what do you do?". No problem. I think that is important too. It's just 2nd. My mission is to make a positive impact on the lives of young people. I serve as a character coach for a men's college basketball program. I also mentor young people and those that influence young people for God's glory. I also serve as a husband to my loving wife Mindy who behind Jesus is my second savior. I also parent and love my son's Austin and Stuart. I support them in their sports and music and journey to discover Jesus. And now God has directed me to write down what I have learned on my journey to hopefully encourage and bring energy to those that are asleep or spiritually dead.

> *Our answer to "who am I" should then describe our character, not our activity.*

You are so much more than what you do. The many things you do are just canvases for you to paint pictures of who you really are and to serve people well.

PRACTICAL PERSPECTIVES TO A TRANSFORMED LIFE

- My life and the things I do are for His glory not mine. What have I been choosing?

- Things happen FOR me not TO me. Everything that happens is in my best interest and an opportunity to learn and grow.

- What life have I been truly missing out on? Rethink fun.

- With Christ, I have enough & I am enough.

- All things are possible with God. With Him, I can do all things.

- My value comes from WHOSE I am first and then who I am. Who I am is my character not my activity.

Chapter 7

A NEW ENDING

"There was a carpenter from England named John. He had built hundreds of houses for his company over the last fifteen years, and his work was so good that the company became one of the most sought after home builders in the country. John worked extremely hard putting in overtime nearly every day, and paying special attention to detail on every project.

After years of dedication, John decided he was going to retire. His boss was very appreciative of the years of diligent service John had given to him and the company. His boss asked if he would build just one more house for a very special friend of his. Half-heartedly, John agreed and began work on the house.

Though he had built excellent houses in the past, this build was different. Many times in the past John had pushed through days and months where he struggled to find motivation, but he just didn't feel it on this project (ever felt like that?). Knowing this was his last go around, John showed up each day with less focus than usual. He bought materials and supplies that were not up to his typical standard. He delegated a lot of tasks without providing supervision. He only worked the hours he was "supposed to," knowing he could build a house up to code basically by going through the motions. He showed up everyday with little joy and without the drive to be better than he was the day before.

Despite the lack of desire and motivation, the house was built on time and was up to code, although not built to the standard he was used to. Walking into the office, beaming ear to ear, John meets with his boss to shake hands and say farewell. After saying thanks, John walks towards the door. His boss calls to him, "John, one last thing." As John turns to face him, his boss hands him a small box with a ribbon around it. John opens the box and pulls out a set of shiny silver keys. His boss says, "Thank you for all you've done for us. The house is yours. You deserve it." His boss had just given him the keys to the house John just built.

Immediately, John's heart sank. If only he knew that he was building his own house, he would have done it all differently. He would have worked with passion and precision. He would have spent twice the amount of time and would have showed up every day with a clear focus on the job at hand, knowing that he was going to reap what he was sowing."[6]

> *We were not born winners or losers… we were born choosers*

We all have a choice. God has given us the blueprints, the plans, for the house He wants us to build. He has given us certain skills that we'll need to build the type of house He wants us to live in. The stage has been set. Are we going to build it to His specs? Are we going to build it His way? Jesus said these words during the sermon on the mount regarding the house we are setting out to build.

"Therefore everyone who <u>hears</u> these words of mine and <u>puts them into practice</u> is like a wise man who built his house on the rock. The rain came down, the streams rose, and the winds blew and beat against that house; yet it did not fall, because it had its foundation on the rock. But everyone who hears these words of mine and does not put them into practice is like a foolish man who built his house on sand. The rain came down, the streams rose, and the winds blew and beat against that house, and it fell with a great crash."

— MATTHEW 7:24-27, NIV WITH ANNOTATION

Houses that stay standing through the storms leave a legacy. They are talked about long after the builder has passed away. They are admired and other houses are modeled after them. Dr. Martin Luther King built one of those houses. Mother Theresa built one of those houses as well. Tony Dungy is another man that is putting the final touches on the house he will leave for us. Billy Graham was quite the builder himself. I want my children to look at my house and want their's to be as durable and resilient as mine.

If I want that, I have to pay attention to how I am building it NOW. There is no time to wait. I am not in control of when my shift is over. The Boss has standards and He also has rewards for those diligent builders. It's time to hear His words and put them into practice. It's time to look in the mirror and when we walk away, remember what we look like. It's time to get off the sidelines and stop allowing the world and pop culture to dictate the way we play the game of life. It's time to stop believing who Jesus was and start trusting who Jesus is. It is time to untangle ourselves from the worldly nets we've been caught in and start following Jesus.

Appendix

40 DAY DAILY DEVOTIONAL

The following section is a daily devotional plan. I mentioned this as one of the HOW's to following Jesus. This will start you on your new journey. It includes a scripture, my perspective and thoughts on it and also a daily commitment for you to keep (to practice) that day.

Each day, read 1 devotional. Read the scripture. Think about what it means or a truth that God is trying to communicate to you. Then read the short commentary. I tried to write about personal experiences that tie my faith with everyday life. At the end, there is a daily commitment for you to adopt. Try to do or believe that thing that day. Remember it. Say it over in your head throughout the day. Post it on social media to hold yourself accountable to it. Finally, pray for the Holy Spirit to guide you in that word that day and be committed to the #TodayIWill statement. If you miss a day, don't freak out. Just pick up where you left off. But the more consistent and committed you are, the more it will shape you.

If you will practice your walk with Christ every day, it will become who you are. I believe if you will read this daily devotion for 40 days, you will see a different person in the mirror at the end.

DAY 1

The Difference the Light Makes

God's Word
"Your word is a lamp to guide my feet and a light for my path" - Psalms 119:105, NLT

How I See It
I got up one morning before the sun came up. Everyone was still asleep. The house was dark. I tried to stay as quiet as possible not to wake up my wife and not turn on any lights as I navigated to the bathroom and eventually downstairs. We have lived in this house for over 13 years. The rooms have had the same configuration, our bedroom furniture has had the same configuration, the path to the closet and around the bed into the bathroom hasn't changed. But in the dark, it's always a challenge to move around without bumping into something.

I see my life like that too. I know what to do to be successful. I know how to talk to people so they feel cared for and important. I know how to serve; I know how to give. I know how I should use my time effectively, and I know that people & relationships are much more important than things and processes. Just like my house layout and the location of my furniture, I know where all of those things are. And in the light, God's guiding light, I flow between them pretty well, without incident. I don't even have the think about what I am doing. It just happens.

But when its dark, it's a whole different ballgame. When I have shaded myself, or turned away from a full-frontal surrender to God, it starts to get dicey. All my focus and attention goes to what I can't see. I put my hands out to warn me of the dresser I am about to run into or the door facing I am about to clip. A place I know and have experienced daily for years becomes difficult and slow in the dark. Same with how I treat others, my willingness to serve and give, and remembering what is most important. When I don't let God's light into those situations, I stumble.

That is why we must stay in the light if we want to go the farthest the fastest. Even when He points us into unfamiliar territory, His light guides the way so we don't have to slow down and feel our way around. Even if we don't see the destination off in the distance, we see the path in front of us clearly when we truly are trusting His light.

My Daily Commitment

#TodayIWill focus on staying in God's light and under His direction even in familiar surroundings

DAY 2

Process Toward Hope

God's Word

"Not only so, but we also glory in our sufferings because we know that suffering produces perseverance; perseverance, character; and character, hope. And hope does not put us to shame, because God's love has been poured out into our hearts through the Holy Spirit, who has been given to us." - Romans 5:3-5, NIV

How I See It

As I really study this, it is saying we can even enjoy our difficulties because of one major reason...HOPE. Pushing through difficulties produces perseverance. And this process builds needed character. And once we have built up character, we inherently then start to have the hope that God is in charge and He is working for my good.

We actually are able to live out Romans 3:5 because we have personally grown into HOPE. And here is the kicker, once we have hope, Paul says HOPE WILL NOT PUT US TO SHAME. Hope signifies that the Holy Spirit (God's love) is living inside of us. Once we have hope, we are unstoppable.

Our walk in this crazy but beautiful world is a process of Troubles > Perseverance > Character > Hope. But once we arrive at a heart posture of hope, it doesn't mean the troubles, perseverance, character building stops. It just means we know the outcome and we can rejoice in the process the rest of our lives.

Where ever we are in the process, know that we are working toward an outcome that will not put us to shame. Hope!

My Daily Commitment

#TodayIWill continue to persevere because I know the trials I am experiencing are necessary ingredients of my ultimate hope

DAY 3

Removing the Debris

God's Word

"Therefore, since we are surrounded by such a huge crowd of witnesses to the life of faith, let us strip off every weight that slows us down, especially the sin that so easily trips us up." - Hebrews 12:1a, NIV

How I See It

Many times we may work hard to put ourselves in positions to hear God's word, be an encouragement to others, or be others focused, but it seems even those good things are not bringing us nor drawing others closer to God. I believe there are unique things in our life that we inadvertently allow to trip us up. These unintentional things that just hang around become debris. This debris blocks the effectiveness of our well-meaning actions. So if there is something restricting the flow of God's love through us, we need to clean it out.

One piece of debris I had to remove was profanity. Words are not just words. They come with a meaning and communicate respect. It's interesting how most of the time we think of our actions not lining up with our words. In my case, my words were not lining up with my actions. And my disrespectful language was a barrier in my relationship with Jesus and poisoning the relationships I was cultivating with other friends. In order to move forward, profanity had to go. All of it.

Another chunk of debris was selfishness. I needed to remove "me" and "my" selfish desires so God could repurpose my time and attention to help others.

By removing debris from my life, it has allowed me to grow closer to who He wants me to be. Consider this morning what debris you need to have the courage to admit you need to clean out in order to allow the spirit to flow through you.

My Daily Commitment

#TodayIWill take the time to examine my heart and identify the debris that is blocking the flow of God's spirit

DAY 4

Rejected

God's Word

"You are coming to Christ, who is the living cornerstone of God's temple. He was rejected by people, but he was chosen by God for great honor." – 1 Peter 2:4, NLT

How I See It

I rejected Christ a good portion of my life. I think I rejected Him largely because I focused on the things I thought He would take away. I heard Travis Crim speak on this one time and he hit the nail on the head. I thought being a "real" Christian (because if you would have asked me back then if I was a Christian I would have told you yes), would mean taking away my fun, friends, and freedom. And because of my immaturity, I didn't want to live without those 3 F's. I have learned a lot about those 3 F's now, that I wish I would have been willing to investigate back then.

It's true, becoming a follower of Christ (aka what I used to call a "real Christian") does remove the destructive path of what I called "fun". I had a warped sense that temporary pleasure was fun. God's fun is long term and does not go away in the morning. I didn't understand I could trade "fun" for deep fulfillment.

It's true, following Christ will remove the "what have you done for me lately "or "love you today hate you tomorrow" friends. A life led in the other direction will attract people who love you for who you are and see the potential in you and encourage you. It prunes the selfish negative influences. And it may even transform them.

Thirdly, yes, it's true. Following Christ does take away the "doing it my way" plan of attack to gaining worldly success and fortune. And replaces it with inspired living utilizing your natural gifts to make a positive impact on others and the world around you. The freedom we think we are giving up is actually saving us from buying a ticket to prison. True freedom is living free of judgement and the opinions of others because you know you have a savior that loves you more than others ever could and will do for you something they never can.

My Daily Commitment

#TodayIWill think about the things I need to give up in order to follow Christ.

DAY 5

Surrender To the Process

"Father, if you are willing, please take this cup of suffering away from me. Yet I want your will to be done, not mine." – Luke 22:42, NLT

How I See It

God is active in the lives of those who surrender to Him. To be more specific, He is always at work, but when we surrender our situations and circumstances to Him, His involvement is obvious and a source of strength in the future.

I've experienced this a number of times. One time was during the process of pursuing my calling. I did not believe I could fully pursue God's calling and run 2 businesses so I decided to sell them both. Not long after I had made the decision, I had a person that was interested in taking over the businesses. We worked diligently with each other sharing information and coming to terms. The day we were supposed to sign a letter of intent, the person backed away from what we had agreed to in our months of discussions. I was back to square one.

My natural instinct was to be mad and extremely disappointed, but I knew what God was calling me into. And He would not bring me this far just to leave me. I came home and told my wife what had happened but expressed to her that God had a plan. I was totally surrendered to God's process rather than my result. Now that I think back to that time, it is amazing how calm and clear and positive I was during a time that would normally cause opposites emotions. I attribute that all to God's spirit telling me to trust in what He was doing.

When we surrender to God's process rather than becoming a prisoner not our specific result, life is a fulfilling journey and we have a front row seat to His glory.

My Daily Commitment

#TodayIWill not become a prisoner to the result that I want. I will gladly surrender to the process God has designed to get me where I need to be.

DAY 6

Transformed In Time

<u>God's Word</u>

"Standing nearby were six stone water jars for the Jewish ceremonial washing. Each could hold twenty or thirty gallons. Jesus told the servants, "Fill the jars with water." When the jars had been filled, he said, "Now dip some out, and take it to the master of ceremonies." So the servants followed his instructions." - John 2:6-8, NLT

<u>How I See It</u>

Transform was my One Word in 2016. Specifically transforming the lives of others through relationship. Relationships are long term. Jesus transformed water into wine in an instant, but I believe He did that to show His power to those close to Him. That He has the power to do the same thing with their ordinary lives but the process will be a little different. It is a longer term plan.

In the book Chop Wood Carry Water by Joshua Medcalf, one of the primary themes is this: on the journey to become the best version of yourself, there are no short cuts. It takes time & devotion to doing the seemingly ordinary tasks to build up the discipline and habits necessary to mold you into who God ultimately wants you to be.

That is my story of transformation. There was no near death experience and the next day I became a sidewalk prophet. It started with a seed that was planted when I was a teenager, lay dormant and actually suppressed through my 20's, and was brought to life again in my late 20's and has grown since. More recent years have been about consistency. Attending church, being open to the truth of the Word, serving, daily reading, being generous, sharing my faith, being consciously aware of what God is trying to accomplish in my life. I am certainly not where I need to be but I'm so glad I am not where I used to be.

A transformed life in Christ has no short cuts. Yes, confessing your sins, asking for forgiveness, and turning toward a life of surrender to His plan can happen in an instant, but that then initiates the process of allowing God to turn us into all He created us to be. It's a whole lot of seemingly ordinary chopping wood and carrying water but what it produces over time is extraordinary.

My Daily Commitment

#TodayIWill not fall victim to the temptation of taking a short cut. Short cuts will leave me short changed.

DAY 7

Acknowledging Adversity

<u>God's Word</u>

"And we know that in all things God works for the good of those who love Him and are called according to His purpose." - Romans 8:28, NIV

<u>How I See It</u>

Today references a verse I have come to strongly believe in and use as a rebuttal to what we tell ourselves (and try to tell God) in the midst of adversity.

When adversity hits, our flesh cries out... this is too hard, I can't do it, life is so unfair, I don't deserve this, I can't ever catch a break, why me, I don't want to go through this. The natural thing is to run and hide or bathe in self pity.

But there is another response that God is calling us to. You know ... those that are called according to His purpose. When the flesh cries out, the holy spirit gives it a tissue and says dry it up. I am bigger than this problem and difficulty. I love you and have a plan for it all. I am working this for your good and no power of hell or scheme of man can alter it.

The more I intentionally pray, read, think, believe, persevere, and stay hopeful in this verse, the more I see it come true. By practicing

& trusting this belief, my eyes are opened to seeing it. But when I complain and become rebellious to the circumstance God is trying to use, it's lights out. I am not going to see the good even when it happens.

May we make a practice of acknowledging difficulty but also acknowledging that our God is bigger than the difficulty. He is working for our good.

<u>My Daily Commitment</u>

#TodayIWill acknowledge the difficulty but embrace the truth that God is working for my good even when it is difficult to see

DAY 8

Put the Salt Water Down

God's Word

"But whoever drinks the water I give them will never thirst. Indeed, the water I give them will become in them a spring of water welling up to eternal life.'" - John 4:14, NIV

How I See It

I read an author say this in a devotional I was reading one day. "My life flourishes when I am rooted in the wisdom and truth of God's word, and when I stay near the living water Jesus offers." There is no doubt that I am most joyful and purposeful when I am following Jesus example. His living water continues to restore and renew.

I read a quote a while back and I wrote it down. I saw it again in a book and it is so applicable to the results produced by the temptations of the world and living outside or away from God's guiding. "Like guzzling salt water, achievement only creates a greater desire to accomplish more, dehydrating us of true satisfaction and fulfillment."

Worldly pursuits never satisfy. No matter how much we consume, it is never enough. You can never have enough money. You can never win enough championships. You can never have a powerful enough position within your organization. The worldly pursuits can never fully satisfy and there is always an emptiness regardless of how much you get. Think back … have you ever said "When I get _____, I'll be so much happier!" After the newness wore off, were you still happy?

So what does fulfill and satisfy? My answer is … the byproducts of surrender. Surrendering your life to a plan that is outside of your control. Acknowledging your gifts, focusing outwardly to serving others, and coming under the authority of Thee not Me.

It is time that we put down the glass of salty water. It is good to gargle when we have a sore throat, but its consumption will never satisfy the thirst we truly have for fulfillment, purpose, peace, and joy.

<u>My Daily Commitment</u>

#TodayIWill surrender my life to a different plan & stop chasing the empty worldly things that I think will satisfy me.

DAY 9

I'd Rather Be Fishing

<u>God's Word</u>

And he said to them, "Follow me, and I will make you fishers of men." - Matthew 4:19, NASB

<u>How I See It</u>

Reading the story about Peter, Andrew, James and John remind me of my teenage years when a buddy and I fished a lot. We had so much fun and really got into it. Through days and days of fishing during the summer, we learned some things. Most importantly, we had to use the right bait. We would shop at the bait store or Walmart to find the bait or lures we thought would catch the fish. Our criteria for selecting bait was 1) did it sound attractive, 2) did it act like something a fish would be attracted to, and 3) once they took the bait, did it taste like something they wanted to keep eating. We would catch the most with baits that were high in these categories.

Fishing for people is very similar. To attract people to Jesus, we are the bait.

1. Do we sound attractive? Do the words that come from our mouths attract people to us or are they often critical and negative turning people away. If our words aren't appealing, not

only will we not catch fish, we won't get them close enough to even be curious. We might even scare them away.

2. Do our actions attract or repel? Are we luring others toward us with caring actions, serving others, being kind and generous? Are we mainly positive and optimistic. Joyful or determined and purposeful when adversity hits us. That's what Jesus' hope creates in us and that is what attracts others. Do we have something that they want for themselves?

3. Once they take the bait, are we real? Are we authentic, kind, consistent! Are we someone they can sink their teeth into? Do we have the characteristics that present us as someone that can be trusted? Or do we feel different once a person touches us, representing one set of morals and ethics on Wednesday morning but another on Friday night? Just like trying to catch a bass on a fake, cheap, off color plastic worm... fish know it is fake and want no part of it and spit it out. People are the same way. They know it's not real so they reject it and keep walking. We've all known people that give a good impression but once you get to know them a little, the inside doesn't match the outside. We don't want to be one of those people.

May we all sound, behave, and continue to live in a manner that draws others to Jesus and be skilled fishers of men.

My Daily Commitment

#TodayIWill live in a way that makes someone want to ask me why I'm different.

DAY 10

Just a Bruise

God's Word

"You were dead because of your sins and because your sinful nature was not yet cut away. Then God made you alive with Christ, for he forgave all our sins." - Colossians 2:13, NLT

How I See It

We have all been bruised by our past. But Jesus stills sees our value and usefulness. This may seem a little funny but this makes me think of bananas. When we buy them in the store, they are pretty perfect and yellow. But by the time we get them home and put them on the counter, they get bruised and develop brown spots.

Our boys see the bananas with spots and see them as damaged and not any good. I see them differently. It is still a good banana; tasty and nutritious. The fact that it has a little bruise doesn't really affect its usefulness.

I think Jesus sees me like that. I started out without blemishes, but over time I got bruised. Mostly of my own doing. But those bruises don't keep me from being useful and serving a purpose. In fact, unlike a banana, Jesus heals those bruises where they are not sensitive anymore. Where there was once a bad spot, He has redeemed them and even the parts that were damaged can be useful again.

May we all be an encouragement to each other to keep seeking God's will for our lives in spite of our bruises.

My Daily Commitment

#TodayIWill not allow a small bruise from my past to keep me from providing value to others

DAY 11

Don't Hide ... Go Seek

God's Word

"In the same way, the Spirit helps us in our weakness. We do not know what we ought to pray for, but the Spirit himself intercedes for us through wordless groans." - Romans 8:26, NIV

How I See It

One of the toughest spiritual disciplines for me is prayer. Am I praying for the right things? Do I believe in my prayers enough? If God's working it out, how important are my prayers. Should I pray for something generic so it is easier to see them answered.

These don't seem like the thoughts of a faithful Christian I begin to think to myself. But then I have another thought. Maybe it's more about the seeking than the finding. Maybe it's more about getting immersed in seeking the will of God (questions and all) and letting His will happen around me.

A picture comes to my mind of when we were kids playing hide and go seek. How many of us would put our hands over our eyes but look through the cracks between our fingers while we counted? That is what i feel like I do in seeking God. Rather than close my eyes and focus on the prayers of my heart, I am constantly peeking with my mind's eye at how those requests are going to work out.

The fruit of my life always seems to be the ripest when I am seeking God without a predetermined agenda. There is a time for specifics as the book Circle Maker by Mark Batterson taught me but there is also a time to seek God's personal presence and peace without a result in mind and (very importantly for me) to be ok with that. Accept what He provides.

<u>My Daily Commitment</u>

#TodayIWill seek God's will without a personal predetermined agenda

DAY 12

Nothing Wasted

<u>God's Word</u>

"There is a time for everything, and a season for every activity under the heavens" - Ecclesiastes 3:1, NIV

<u>How I See It</u>

I need reminders often that there is a season for everything. We all go through seasons. Some of our choosing and some not. And just because we choose it doesn't mean it is a comfortable season. It would seem to reason that anything you choose would be a good season and anything unexpected would be a bad season. That's not the case because we are not always good choosers :-)

But something that I need to tattoo on the top of my hand so it is always in front of me is that God is with us in every season. No matter the prosperity or struggle, He is there.

Being totally vulnerable, I have been in season where I have asked God why He has me wasting my time where I was`. It felt so fruitless and unimportant. But His word says there is a season for everything. Even a season of no visible fruit and no visible meaning. But just because I don't see it, doesn't mean God isn't using it. I just means He isn't allowing me to see it.

I have to remind myself that God wastes nothing. What seems dry and barren is just that way because of the filter and perspective I see it through. We have to battle the thoughts that it is wasted time. Rather than ask "why I am here" it is better to ask "what are you teaching me here".

My Daily Commitment

#TodayIWill be content in my current season realizing God wastes nothing.

DAY 13

Fix It

God's Word

"You can make many plans, but the Lord's purpose will prevail." - Proverbs 19:21

How I See It

We all have had our encounter with brokenness. No matter how we were raised, how much money we have, where we live, how many people love us, even involvement in a fulfilling ministry. Our lives are not immune from brokenness.

But man, I'm a fixer. Identify the problem, brainstorm solution, make a decision, and execute the fix. That works well with lawn mower handles and business processes. It doesn't work very well for people.

In our hands and under our direction, handles and processes are within our control. No matter how much we hate it or how hard we try, we cannot control other people. It frustrates us to no end. We see the problem, we see the fix. But we are not in control of the execution.

That's when we have to surrender it to God. He is the only one that has the power to bring the dead back to life. Not long ago, our pastor said something that really applies to my thoughts today. Jesus did not come to make bad people, good people. He came to make dead people alive. Brokenness in many situations is tied to sin which breeds death. So Jesus came to restore brokenness. Make dead people alive again.

When we or someone we know is broken, God is the ultimate fix. No schemes or promises, change of location or tax bracket, can have the restorative power to heal and fix like Jesus. May we lift our friends, families, acquaintances, leaders, or maybe even ourselves to the Lord today and ask Him to make clear the brokenness so He can come in and apply the fix.

My Daily Commitment

#TodayIWill be aware of my areas of brokenness to enable God's love to fix it.

DAY 14

Spring Cleaning

"The mind governed by the flesh is death, but the mind governed by the Spirit is life and peace." - Romans 8:6, NIV

How I See It

Weeding out negativity in our minds is a necessary and worthy task. Sometimes the negative thoughts start to overtake the positive ones just like an untended garden or flower bed.

In my own flower beds, I don't prioritize it and they get out of control. Then one day I see how ugly it looks. And I am convicted that something has to be done. At that point, I jump in there and start cleaning up.

My life kind of works like that too. I prioritize others things and allow the weeds to grow. They are not a big deal at first. It's like I accept them as a piece of the puzzle. But then more and more pop up and finally I look at myself and say wow, that is ugly. I've got to get my mind/heart cleaned up.

Some thoughts are easy to pull out. They don't have deep roots and are easy to discard. But others have much deeper roots and it takes a tool to extract. Tools like scripture verses such as Proverbs 3:5 and Philippians 4:8 and Romans 8:28. Other tools are reading books written by people such as Jon Gordon, Mark Batterson, Jamie Gilbert, & Andy Andrews. Yet another tool is putting myself around people that plant so many positive thoughts that it actually chokes out the negative.

It's time to put on the work clothes today and go pull some weeds.

<u>My Daily Commitment</u>

#TodayIWill notice the weeds I have let grow in my life and start the process of pulling them up.

DAY 15

A Tool to Grow Us, Not Destroy Us

God's Word

Then he said to them, "My soul is overwhelmed with sorrow to the point of death. Stay here and keep watch with me." - Matthew 26:38, NIV

How I See It

God reminded me of something profound one Sunday morning during worship. I have been very negative about suffering. I guess we would all agree that suffering is seen as negative and grim. I could not connect suffering with my Christian Faith. Christian Faith is about hope and a future. Character and overcoming. Positive things!

And then it hit me out of the blue. Jesus suffered. As He sat in the garden of Gethsemane, he was struggling. He was suffering emotionally about what was about to happen. It was going to hurt, be humiliating, and I want to think that Jesus had a brief moment where He thought "I could do a ton more good down here. Don't cut it short Dad." Jesus suffered emotionally, mentally, & physically.

That is why we can trust God through our suffering. Because He knows how we feel. He's been there. It has been a piece of this world since its creation, but Jesus experienced it in order to have credibility that it can be overcome. Because He overcame it! We can experience it and know suffering is not be the end of the story.

So let us not be ashamed or feel like we are giving false hope when we encourage others through suffering. Suffering is a component of our faith and a tool to grow us, not destroy us. May Jesus be our example to live through the suffering!

My Daily Commitment

#TodayIWill look at suffering in a new light. It is necessary as a tool to grow us, not destroy us.

DAY 16

Deal With It or Done With It

<u>God's Word</u>

On hearing this, Jesus said to them, "It is not the healthy who need a doctor, but the sick. I have not come to call the righteous, but sinners." - Mark 2:17, NIV

<u>How I See It</u>

Since I was a kid, I have had pretty bad allergies. Stuffy and runny nose has been a staple of my life it seems. As I've gotten older, I've just kind of dealt with it. Sudafed, Benadryl, and Afrin have become part of my diet like chicken fingers and sweet tea.

Over the years, infection has set in and my health has gotten worse. It moves from being an annoyance (and probably annoyance for those around me too) to a condition that is affecting my ability to function at the level I want and need to. But many times, even though I KNOW it has gotten worse, I still try to treat it the same way. I try to ignore it and hope it gets better. I push through under the belief that I am tough and I don't have time for this. The show must go on. But eventually, when I cannot take it any longer and I feel miserable, I go to the doctor.

We all get physically sick every now and then, but one sickness that we were born with is sin. In our early years, it starts to creep in like a runny nose and we just deal with it. But the longer it lasts and the more involved we get, it becomes a bigger problem. We become infected with sin and it starts to affect our relationships, job, self-esteem, confidence, and even our faith in Jesus. And in our zeal to be tough and push through, we try to treat it with worldly medicines of making more money, cheating to get ahead, spending more hours at work, mind altering substances, and other things. We eventually find out we are tired of just temporarily feeling better. We want to be healed.

The sickness of sin can only be healed by the great physician, Jesus. His love, acceptance, forgiveness, and redemption is the only cure for the sickness that sin causes. As with a physical sickness, we have to come to the point where we realize we need the doctor. Jesus is not going to kick down your door, hold you down, and inject you with the vaccination. Although his office is open 24/7, it's our choice and decision to come see him. And He does make house calls. But again, you've got to call out to him in prayer and invite Him in so you can begin to get well. Have you been dealing with the ongoing sickness of sin and are finally ready to be healed today?

<u>My Daily Commitment</u>

#TodayIWill acknowledge that I am sick and need to allow the doctor to heal me. No more trying to tough it out on my own.

DAY 17

Modeling the Gospel

<u>God's Word</u>

"Therefore go and make disciples of all nations, baptizing them in the name of the Father and of the Son and of the Holy Spirit, and teaching them to obey everything I have commanded you. And surely I am with you always, to the very end of the age." - Matthew 28:19-20, NIV

<u>How I See It</u>

There are times when I really struggle with the great commission and just loving people for who they are. The great commission in Matthew 28:19-20 says "Therefore go and make disciples of all nations, baptizing them in the name of the Father and of the Son and of the Holy Spirit, and teaching them to obey everything I have commanded you. And surely I am with you always, to the very end of the age."

I take this as evangelism. Which I then translate to approaching people with questions about their belief in Jesus and subsequent explanation of what a personal relationship with Jesus has done in my own life. But as I read this great commission, in verse 20 it says "teaching" them to obey everything I have commanded you.

One way to teach is to tell. Explain verbally. Another way to teach is to model. Explain through action.

When it comes to people of different faiths and beliefs, I think our most effective method is to model love not just tell someone about it. We model love by being kind, serving, and being willing to listen. Respecting their observances while not compromising our own. That is what Jesus has commanded us in John 13:34, "Love one another". Love is a verb, an action, not just a word.

Making disciples of all nations seems unrealistic honestly as I look at the world today. But the disciples probably thought the same thing and look at us now! The whole world has not been made a disciple but their effort has made great progress in this world and I am thankful for them pressing on. Who is going to be unknowingly thankful for the love we showed others and how we played a role in advancing the kingdom one day?

My Daily Commitment

#TodayIWill spread the Gospel showing unconditional love & respect to those around me regardless of their beliefs and traditions.

DAY 18

Perfect Parent

God's Word

"Endure hardship as discipline; God is treating you as his children. For what children are not disciplined by their father?" - Hebrews 12:7, NIV

How I See It

I believe God is a perfect parent. Protecting and nurturing us through life. There is a time when we do need to intercede and make sacrifices for our children. But certainly not save them 100% of the time from the consequences of their own choices or even the consequences of decisions that were made for them.

And just like a perfect parent, God disciplines his children. When we choose to be disobedient, we must be disciplined. Discipline many times is experiencing the consequences of our actions. God disciplines us (His children) just like a good parent disciplines their child.

But just like our perfect parent, there is a time when we must be ushered out of the safety of our childhood nest and learn to build our own nest. Learn to build our own life, make our own choices, navigate the consequences of our choices, and establish our own faith journey. But our perfect parent is still always there for us for advice, support, encouragement, and love. And when we falter, that perfect parent is there to pick us up and set our feet back on the path. That is what loving earthly parents do for their children.

I believe a perfect parent on earth is like our perfect parent above. He loves us unconditionally and desires the best for us, but also understands to be the strongest we can be, we must learn to fight our own battles and make our own choices. That's what God does for us.

My Daily Commitment

#TodayIWill let those I love fight their own battles.

DAY 19

Know How You Feel

God's Word

"For we do not have a high priest who is unable to empathize with our weaknesses, but we have one who has been tempted in every way, just as we are--yet he did not sin." - Hebrews 4:15, NIV

How I See It

Today's scripture is a point I think we often lose sight of. Jesus knows how we feel. He saw & experienced the world up close and personal. We experience the pain, shame, guilt, and nastiness of just <u>our</u> sin. While unpleasant, that seems fair right?

Jesus felt the pain & nastiness of EVERYBODY'S sin and did it with the public humiliation on a cross and nails. Have you ever felt the pain and embarrassment caused by the sin of a loved one? Doesn't seem fair does it? Jesus knows how we feel.

He felt rejection. He felt doubted. He felt alone. He felt betrayed.

He too felt the sting of obedience. Luke 22:42 says "Father, if you are willing, take this cup from me; yet not my will, but yours be done."

No matter our sin or circumstance, Jesus is there with us and He knows how we feel. We should not run from Jesus when we are damaged by sin but rather run to Him because He knows how we feel and will be the one for sure that will not cast judgement on us, shame us, guilt us, or make us feel worse. Running to Jesus provides forgiveness which enables us to return to who He wants us to be!

<u>My Daily Commitment</u>

#TodayIWill not feel alone in my pain or doubt because I understand that Jesus knows how I feel.

DAY 20

What Are You Feeding You

God's Word

"For God did not give us a spirit of fear timidity, but of power, love, and self-discipline" - 2 Timothy 1:7, NLT

How I See It

My favorite verse about fear is 2 Timothy 1:7. You just read it above. It may seem obvious from that verse but I want to say it again very clearly. Fear does not come from God. It originates from sin and satan. So in the face of uncertainty or danger, we choose to allow 1 of 2 things to drive our thoughts and attitudes. Either a spirit of fear OR a spirit of love, power, and self-control. And the spirit we choose to listen to then drives our behavior.

In Jon Gordon's book the Energy Bus, he writes about a man that feels like he has 2 dogs inside of him. One dog is vicious, mean, selfish, fearful and overall negative. The other is loving, optimistic, disciplined, and very positive. The 2 dogs fight within this man all the time. He seeks out a wise man to ask him which dog he thinks will win. His response was the one you feed. So feed the positive dog.

In each one of us, there is a fearful dog and a loving, powerful dog. The one that is going to win is the one we feed. Don't make fear our choice. Let's feed ourselves scripture, memories of God's faithfulness in our own lives, stories about other overcomers, other encouraging thoughts and beliefs.   And realize that sometimes we just have to demand of ourselves, despite the circumstances, I am not going to be afraid.

Let's choose faith over fear today and feed our faith all day!

<u>My Daily commitment</u>

#TodayIWill make a choice to focus on positive, encouraging things to feed my faith.

DAY 21

Discomfort of Obedience

God's Word

"In their hearts humans plan their course, but the LORD establishes their steps." - Proverbs 16:9, NIV

How I See It

Many times, when things don't go according to our plans, it is caused by circumstances outside of our control. That is confusing for sure and requires us to trust God's plan.

But what about when things don't go according to our plans and our intentional choices are the cause of the deviation? I'm not sure what is harder to reconcile, a change of plan due to unforeseen circumstances or a change in plan due to obedience to God's call.

Bottom line is a change in plan causes doubt and unrest. You would think there would be great comfort in knowing your discomfort is being caused by obedience. But obedience doesn't remove the discomfort. I believe it does though provide hope. 1 Peter 3:17 says "For it is better, if it is God's will, to suffer for doing good than for doing evil." Not that sudden circumstances are evil, but it does touch on the pain of obedience.

I tell people this often when I am asked about purpose and their future. God wants us to be where He wants us to be even more than we want us to be where He wants us to be. I think holding onto that promise is the key to managing any change of plan, whether sudden or intentional. He knows the path to that mystical, spiritual place better than we do and we have to do our best to follow the directions we feel He has given.

Thanks for being on the follower's journey with me and many others. Pray the thoughts and scriptures in this book are making a difference in your life and the people around you.

My Daily Commitment

#TodayIWill trust that God is guiding me to my next milestone whether it was part of my plan or not.

DAY 22

Don't Block A Blessing

God's Word

"When Moses' hands grew tired, they took a stone and put it under him and he sat on it. Aaron and Hur held his hands up—one on one side, one on the other—so that his hands remained steady till sunset." - Exodus 17:12, NIV

How I See It

This is a lesson that took me a while to learn and still sometimes forget. It's ok to ask for help. And not only is it ok to ask for help, we could actually be blocking a blessing by not asking for help.

Here is what I mean. For years, I didn't want to inconvenience someone else by asking for their help. I thought to myself, "They are busy and have their own problems." But I finally realized I would get frustrated with other people for not asking for my help. I wanted to help them and feel useful. One day I looked in the mirror and it was revealed to me that I was doing the same thing.

We all know how fulfilled we feel when we help others. So by not asking for help, we are not giving others opportunities to serve. And if we do not give others opportunities to serve, we are lessening their opportunities to experience blessings. So when we ask for help, we are actually providing a conduit for a blessing. We are blessed because we get the help we need and the other person is blessed because they were helpful. It is truly a win/win situation.

So now I am much more willing to ask for help because I now see the blessing circle that asking for help completes. Can you see how your well-intentioned thinking of not bothering or inconveniencing others by asking for their help may have blocked a blessing?

My Daily Commitment

#TodayIWill complete the blessing circle by asking others for help.

DAY 23

What Do You See

God's Word

"The eyes of the Lord are everywhere, keeping watch on the wicked and the good." - Proverbs 15:3, NIV

How I See It

I really wonder why we are naturally attracted to bad and negative things? I don't watch the news anymore because it is reporting mostly on what is wrong with the world or our community. To see how natural this is, we can reference the Bible. Even Matthew reported on the evil that was at work during Jesus birth. Matthew is the only book that tells of the account of Jesus birth that adds the back story of King Herod and the order to kill all children less than 2 years old.

But if we use the Gospels as gauge, 4 out of 4 reported the good and 1 out of 4 reported the bad. I think that is a more appropriate ratio for our own lives. 75% positive/good to enable us to be the best we can be and 25% challenging/tough in order to continue to strength us through adversity and stay diligent in doing good. If everything was 100% great all the time, we would not need hope ...

So a good story to offset the local news ... I was at a local charitable organization called Kids to Love one day. Kids To Love serves foster children in north Alabama and southern Tennessee. In addition to serving the needs of foster children and the foster families throughout the year, they provide Christmas for over a 1,000 children. Most of their items are donated new toys and clothes. This particular Christmas season, their donations were up 30% over the previous year. Their warehouse was jammed and they had bikes parked all in every hallway, new toys in their conference rooms, and volunteers working from 7 AM to midnight wrapping presents that would be delivered throughout the region in plenty of time for Christmas. It was an incredible picture of what is good & right around us and the power a Christian woman with a vision to serve has to affect good.

To me, it boils down to choosing to focus on what is right with the world and not what is wrong. Jesus is about hope, Satan is all about stealing, killing, and destroying. I choose hope today even in the face of evil. Evil may win a battle but Hope wins the war. Let's look for good around us.

<u>My Daily Commitment</u>

#TodayIWill choose to look for the good that is going on around me rather than the bad.

DAY 24

A Life of Practice

God's Word

"Keep putting into practice all you learned and received from me—
everything you heard from me and saw me doing. Then the God of
peace will be with you." - Philippians 4:9, NLT

How I See It

Following Christ is a skill. All skills take practice to master and any
time you are practicing something towards mastery, if you are
giving it your best effort, you are occasionally going to fail.

To become a master follower, there are a number of things I need to
practice. I need to be reading scripture consistently, I need to have
a compassionate heart to help those in need, I need to have an
expectant and active prayer life, I need to look beyond my own self-
interest and humble myself to alternate plans. There are more, but
this is a pretty good start.

But the reality of daily life is we are going to encounter failure while
practicing. It may be a busy morning getting the kids off to school
and making a morning meeting that prevents us from being able to
execute on serving others (like happens to me!). It may be having
money in your wallet but you drive by the homeless person.
Occasionally it's just a bunch of prayers for help and not including
the thanks. These are all failures in practice. But the most important

thing is … are we aware of our failures and are we allowing them to nudge us in a higher direction.

One day, I saw a homeless man at an intersection. He had a cardboard sign that read "Any $ helps. God Bless." I had a $20 bill and 2 $1 bills in my wallet. The thoughts rushed through my head as he walked down the row of waiting cars. "Do I give him something? How much? Do I leave any cash for the rest of my drive? I wonder how he feels walking along with this sign. Is he a con that's too lazy to get a job? Lord, what's the right thing to do?"

I got the 2 $1 bills out of my wallet, rolled down the window and gave them to him. But I also looked him in the eye and shook his hand and told him God Bless him. I wanted him to know that I saw him as a person, wasn't afraid to reach out and touch him, and was a friend of God's. Should I have given him the $20 and the 2 $1's? Probably. Should I have reached my hand out of the window and shook his hand? Was that risky? Probably.

But this is the failure and triumphs of following Jesus in a 30 second snapshot of life. Following Jesus is a constant tug of war with ourselves that hopefully the angel on the right shoulder gets the upper hand over the devil on the left. But it's our willingness to work, put in the practice that teaches us how to do it better.

My Daily Commitment

#TodayIWill lovingly look a stranger in the eye and shake their hand or hug their neck. This type of practice makes perfect.

DAY 25

What Needs Healing First

God's Word

"Some people brought to him a paralyzed man on a mat. Seeing their faith, Jesus said to the paralyzed man, "Be encouraged, my child! Your sins are forgiven."" - Matthew 9:2, NLT

How I See It

In the story of the paralyzed man being healed, It's important to notice what Jesus knew needed to be healed first... The man's heart. He does not heal the man's paralysis immediately, first He forgives his sins.

Our paralysis comes in many forms. We think we need to walk again, or be cured of cancer, or be free from debt, repair a shattered relationship, free us from addiction, or regain a client, or win more games. Regardless of our hardship (paralysis), to be personally forgiven is our true need.

God can do all those circumstantial things. But until we experience the depth of God's love and forgiveness, all those other things are not going to give us the freedom we think they will provide.

Jesus was sending the message that our heart needs to be healed first before we can be freed from the paralysis of our circumstances.

May we humbly accept His forgiveness so we may be healed of our afflictions.

My Daily Commitment

#TodayIWill ask Jesus to heal my heart before we changes my circumstances.

DAY 26

Where is Our Shelter

God's Word

"My heart pounds in my chest. The terror of death assaults me. Fear and trembling overwhelm me, and I can't stop shaking. Oh, that I had wings like a dove; then I would fly away and rest! I would fly far away to the quiet of the wilderness. How quickly I would escape - far from this wild storm of hatred." - Psalm 55:4-8, NLT

How I See It

We are all touched by storms of life. They are extremely uncomfortable, scary, angry times. Reading another translation of the scripture today written by the psalmist sounded familiar to me.

55:4 My heart is in anguish within me, the terrors of death have fallen upon me.
55:5 Fear and trembling come upon me, and horror overwhelms me.
55:6 And I say, "O that I had wings like a dove! I would fly away and be at rest;
55:7 truly, I would flee far away; I would lodge in the wilderness; [Selah]
55:8 I would hurry to find a shelter for myself from the raging wind and tempest."

I would be willing to bet that we all have told ourselves similar things at a point in our life. Fear, feelings of being overwhelmed, running away. What we do next is the key though. Where do we seek comfort?

Unfortunately, many times we run and hide in things that only intensify the storm. Abuse of alcohol, drugs, inappropriate relationships. Maybe we run away from home, maybe we run back home. Sometimes we just absorb ourselves in our jobs to shelter us from our personal storms. There are so many escapes that all have something in common. They never provide peace. They may provide temporary comfort or distraction or escape, but they never bring peace.

Jesus's care, sovereignty, and love is what provides peace. In those moments of fear and overwhelming, grabbing the bible rather than the bottle is the solution. Crying out in prayer rather than popping the pill. Considering how bold and courageous Jesus was during His storm can provide the strength to persevere ours. Running from our problems never solves them. Running toward Jesus with our problems can. Lord may we have the integrity and awareness given by your holy spirit to be calm during the storm and make the right decisions.

My Daily Commitment

#TodayIWill not seek comfort and shelter in temporary places. Peace from the storm is only found in Jesus.

DAY 27

Potential to Power

<u>God's Word</u>

"For we are God's masterpiece. He has created us anew in Christ Jesus, so we can do the good things he planned for us long ago." - Ephesians 2:10, NLT

<u>How I See It</u>

God created us all with the capacity to do great things. That's what I call potential. We all have a responsibility to tap into that capacity aka potential. It is there, waiting to be brought out. So why doesn't it get tapped many times?

I believe one reason is we are blind to ourselves. We think we do not have the proper influence, aren't in the right position, don't know enough, don't have as much experience as we need. We come up with all the reasons why we can't do something rather than the 1 reason we could do something. Many times, we just don't see it even though it's there. We need to be willing and obedient to do what we can and see where that leads. Do the 1 thing, no matter how small or weird, that we know how to do to begin to knock on the door of our potential.

Another reason I think we don't tap into our potential is we know it is going to be hard work. Nothing worthwhile ever comes about easy. And it is easier to coast along with comfortable than accelerate through challenge and uncertainty for something better.

In my life, I have grappled with potential. How do I push the envelope to achieve more but not achieve more selfishly, but achieve more in the lives of those around me? I have been comfortable with speaking periodically to athletic teams and youth groups, writing some, engaging in social media positively. But is there more to do. Are there things that I can do to continually realize the full potential God has installed in me. Those decisions are risky and uncomfortable. They are frustrating sometimes, I'm not going to lie, and full of doubt. But we cannot be afraid to engage the challenge and do something new. I love the quote "in order to get something you've never had; you've got to do something you've never done". We are equipped for impact on this world. We've got to be willing to say yes to the 1 thing we can do rather than the 5 we can't AND realize it is going to be hard, but it is going to be worth it.

The greatest reward ends up being who we become on the journey rather than what we accomplish at the destination. Every one of us has potential for great things. Acknowledge it and be willing to put in the work to give others the benefit of it.

<u>My Daily Commitment</u>

#TodayIWill not be afraid to acknowledge the things I CAN do and engage that regardless of how hard it may seem.

DAY 28

Halfway There

God's Word

"And I am certain that God, who began the good work within you, will continue his work until it is finally finished on the day when Christ Jesus returns." - Philippians 1:6, NLT

How I See It

Today is about transitions. We encounter transitions all the time. We are transitioning into a new week. Some are transitioning back to school. Others are transitioning from an off season to game season. Even others may be transitioning from a place of chaos to a place of peace. We have probably all transitioned from being in a relationship to being out of a relationship. I even think of transitioning from a winning streak to a losing streak or losing streak to a winning streak.

Whatever the situation, we are constantly moving from one place to another physically, emotionally, or even spiritually. And in that "in between" we may be looking for God. I really encourage you to read scripture each morning as yet again, I read a verse today from Genesis that has the power to speak into so many situations in my life and especially the transitions.

Genesis 28:15-16 says "I am with you and will watch over you wherever you go, and I will bring you back to this land. I will not leave you until I have done what I have promised you. When Jacob awoke from his sleep, he thought, "Surely the Lord is in this place, and I was not aware of it.""

That is one promise that I tell myself often and remind others in times of transition. God's not going to leave you halfway there. Have you ever considered God's integrity? He is solid in that area. He doesn't break promises and He doesn't do things half way. He finishes what He starts. So as we think about transitions, that implies that we are in between. Not where we were and not quite where we need to be. We are moving from one place to another. But feel confident that there is an end in mind. And a powerful God able to move mountains and part seas has the vision and capability to get you there if you will trust Him.

My Daily Commitment

#TodayIWill believe that God is not done with me yet and He has not brought me to this point to leave me here.

DAY 29

Joy is the Currency

God's Word

"In his grace, God has given us different gifts for doing certain things well. So if God has given you the ability to prophesy, speak out with as much faith as God has given you. If your gift is serving others, serve them well. If you are a teacher, teach well. If your gift is to encourage others, be encouraging. If it is giving, give generously. If God has given you leadership ability, take the responsibility seriously. And if you have a gift for showing kindness to others, do it gladly." - Romans 12:6-8, NLT

How I See It

The title of this message invokes a ton of thoughts and emotions for me. I am asked to volunteer for a lot of things. It is humbling and an honor, but honestly, I say no a lot. I want to be joyful in my serving. Mainly because joy is awesome, but another reason is joy is the reward. Joy is the currency of volunteering. When something brings you joy, that joy spills out. When something becomes work, you lose joy, and the people you are serving or receive the benefit from your service aren't as blessed. And you aren't blessed.

I think it is so important to understand what our gifts are and where we are divinely called. I think followers don't spend enough time or time at all really understanding their gifts. And nothing riles me up more than someone that says they are not good at anything or they don't have any gifts. The second piece of that puzzle is spending enough time in prayer about where we are called.

A couple of years ago, I spent time writing down what I believe my gifts to be. I also spent time in prayer, thought, and reading about calling. When I align my volunteering to my gifts and calling, I wouldn't trade it for any amount of money in the world.

Joy is the currency of volunteering. Joy is the greatest when we are aligning with the gifts God gave us in the area we believe we are called to serve. This could be geographic, with a specific age, gender, income level, job type, industry, sport, or could be a specific type of activity. Areas of calling are as broad as the imagination. Alignment is the key to maximizing joy.

If you have not spent time with calling or understanding your gifts, invest in yourself. A book that was very practical in helping me write and inventory my gifts was 40 Days to Work You Love by Dan Miller. A good book that kicked off my calling journey was The Call by Oz Guinness. If this message today has stirred something within and you don't know where to start, there you go.

My Daily Commitment

#TodayIWill make time to WRITE DOWN what I believe my gifts are & pray for God to lead me to a place of serving with those gifts. (If you will actually do this, it will pay off big for you I promise)

DAY 30

Recharge Your Battery

God's Word

"Do not conform to the pattern of this world, but be transformed by the renewing of your mind. Then you will be able to test and approve what God's will is—his good, pleasing and perfect will." - Romans 12:2, NIV

How I See It

Our cell phone is relevant and identifiable analogy to our faith and our lives. My iPhone can do all kinds of helpful things, but once the battery dies, it's useless. In order for it to be useful again, it must be recharged. And the more we use it (i.e. the more engaged we are in life) the quicker it runs down. Typically, we charge our phones once a day but sometimes we may need to charge it twice or 3 times.

God's word, prayer, and Godly men and women in our life act as those chargers for our soul. The encouragement, challenge, perspective, and prayer those chargers provide is what gets us back going and useful again. I use a devotional each morning to be my morning charge, but I need a boost throughout the day. During the day, it's common to get a text or email, see a tweet, Facebook or Instagram post that provides me a reminder that reorients my day and gives me the boost for the remainder of the day. I experience frustration some days or just get tired. This topic is so real because we experience it almost daily.

And we cannot try to fill back up on ungodly things. It's like plugging up to a bad charger. It's plugged up, but no juice is flowing. Everything looks good to the outside, but nothing is being accomplished.

We all need recharging. If you are pouring out, you need to be filled back up. There is nothing wrong with taking care of yourself. Your mind is going to try to tell you are being selfish. Don't listen to that lie. Say no today so you can say yes tomorrow and not only yes tomorrow, but be charged up and able to give your everything.

My Daily Commitment

#TodayIWill recognize when I am run down and recharge by spiritual battery with prayer and God's word.

DAY 31

Hard to Love

God's Word

"Whoever loves discipline loves knowledge, but whoever hates correction is stupid." - Proverbs 12:1, NIV

How I See It

Being totally honest, I get frustrated at people who are negative, dishonest, lazy, "know it all's" rather than do it all's. My first response is to move past them. My gut reaction is … there is someone else around me that wants to do good, that is truthful, that is hard working, and puts their noses down and goes to work. Those are the people I want to support, those are the people I want to encourage, those are the people that are trying their best to better themselves. Those are the people I want to love and actually spend more time loving.

But as I think about it, love comes in many different forms. A while back, I helped a friend of mine talk through ideas and develop strategies to handle a difficult situation with her team. Some of the players were engaging in behaviors that were detrimental to the team, negatively affecting the program from the locker room to the games. They were doing things that I would say made them hard to love. And even though they were family (in the team sense), they were hard to love because of the divisiveness and disruption it caused to team chemistry. And while my friend cared for them deeply, she was exactly like me... would rather spend more time with the ones that are easier to love.

Love comes in different forms. And God loves us in different ways. God hugs and comforts and he also rebukes and disciplines. Both are love. When we are talking about loving others, I think our minds automatically go to the hugs and comfort types. But that is not the only way and should not be the only way. Sometimes really loving someone is letting them experience the consequences of their choices. It doesn't feel good but that is loving them for the long haul. That is loving them so much that you care about their future as much as their feelings.

This seems like we are getting out of treating someone nicely when they don't "deserve" it. But it's not. Love is deeper and more complex than touchy, feely good stuff. Sometimes love is messy and hard.

So the next time I think about someone being hard to love, I need to understand the depth of love and apply the appropriate love to their situation.

My Daily Commitment

#TodayIWIll not shy away from loving someone enough to let them experience the consequences of their actions

DAY 32

Will It Be a Lie or the Truth?

God's Word

"If we claim to have fellowship with him and yet walk in the darkness, we lie and do not live out the truth." - 1 John 1:6, NIV

How I See It

Today we reflect on growing older. How well am I growing older? Am I continuing to grow closer to God just like a tree grows closer to heaven? Are my roots spreading out farther away from my core family and friends and reaching others in a positive way? Are they not only spreading out but getting deeper into a soil rich with integrity, love, perspective, honesty, and courage? This is how we were made to grow older.

I did an exercise a couple of years ago where I wrote my own obituary. I had to write down what I hoped would be said at my funeral. The point was, how I treated people, where I spent my time, what I valued, my work ethic towards those things I valued was providing the speakers at my funeral all the information on what they would actually say. I have a great influence over that obituary. How I want to be remembered is in direct relationship to how I live in the present.

I do not want to live a lie. The reality is no family member in their grief or speaker at a funeral is going to trash me or anyone else 3 days after they die. They are typically going to pull out the script that says all the right respectful things. He was a loving family man, hard worker, always willing to help those in need, dedicated member of his church, never met a stranger, on and on. The script varies some of course, but the general tone of a southern funeral is the same. So the question is … are we ok living a lie or will that be the truth?

Another thing is nobody really cares how you started, it's all about how you finish. Let me temper that a little. The people you hurt in the beginning will care, but if you finish well, they will most likely forgive. But others that have experienced our strong finish won't give a hoot about the mistakes we made in the past or some scars that we are living with. All they remember is how we made them feel and the positive impact we made on the world in our 2nd half.

<u>My Daily Commitment</u>

#TodayIWill live in a way that prevents people from having to lie at my funeral.

DAY 33

Practice in What Matters

God's Word

"Therefore everyone who hears these words of mine and puts them into practice is like a wise man who built his house on the rock." - Matthew 7:24, NIV

How I See It

To get good at anything takes practice. Practice is intentionally and repetitively going through an activity in order to become proficient in it. I am not sure if that is the dictionary definition but when i think of practice, that is what I would say it is. So, as we strive to be our best, it takes practice. Our best is made up of so many practical components across many different aspects of our lives.

Being a good athlete takes practice. You can't get in shape by running a mile on the first day of workouts and calling it good. It takes intentional, repetitive running to get in shape. There are many great books that tell you how to swing a golf club in order to hit it high and long. But I have never seen a golfer hoist a trophy at any level of competition that spent more time reading about the swing that intentionally and repetitively swinging. To achieve great things, you have to put in the work.

And to be in harmony with God's will, it takes practice. One of the activities that is required is rest. I humbly admit this has been a tough one for me over the years. I am a very driven person and idleness seems like I am wasting valuable time that I could be getting something done. But what I have realized is there is a difference between staying busy and getting stuff done. I can stay busy and make myself feel like I am productive but what I am really producing. If I want to produce lasting, meaningful product, it requires resting in the Lord. Spending quiet time with Him in prayer. Reading the Word. Observing people. Listening rather than talking. Getting enough sleep!

I previously lived a life at 100 mph thinking that if I go fast, I'll go far. That statement is actually true. If I would have kept up that pace and perspective, I would have gone far. The problem is I would have gone WAY down a road and to a place I really didn't want to be. Slowing down and resting in the Lord enables us to still go far, but it takes us to a place of peace and purpose and producing things that really matter.

Practice resting today.

<u>My Daily Commitment</u>

#TodayIWill slow down and take a break from my busyness so I can assess that I am heading down the most beneficial road

DAY 34

Treasure

<u>God's Word</u>

"Where your treasure is, there your heart will be also." - Matthew 6:21, NIV

<u>How I See It</u>

I have often heard this verse and the subject of storing up our treasures in heaven. And then the relationship between our treasure and our heart. I honestly never quite got it. The probable reason is I had not put in enough time considering it and meditating on it. But an event occurred one night that helped provide me with clarity as I reconsidered this verse.

A fellow brother's house was damaged in a fire. While some of their stuff was destroyed along with a couple of rooms of their house, his wife and young son were fine. The verse in Matthew contrasts us storing up treasures in heaven vs storing up treasure on earth. As I heard about the incident and read this verse, it became clearer to me.

We are tempted to put an unhealthy value on things of this earth. And the verse says where our treasure is, so too is our heart. When we value material things and get wrapped up in those things, we become vulnerable to being crushed. Like an unexpected tragedy of a fire, it will take those away. And scripture says our heart will be in those things too, thus our heart will be crushed as well.

But the treasures we store up in heaven can never be taken away. Treasures like our love for each other, the fruit that comes from serving others, our trust and belief in Jesus, confidence in our purpose on this earth. Those are heavenly things. And those are treasures that we should value. Those are also treasures that cannot be taken away. That is where we should desire our heart to be. Our heart should be on heavenly things that cannot be crushed and cannot be taken away.

My heart goes out to their family as they exert energy towards rebuilding and repairing their home on top of the other tasks that were already on their plate. But I also offer them the perspective that the pictures may have been burned and destroyed, but the people in those pictures are alive and well. We can take more pictures and build new houses, but we cannot replace people. Trust in the Lord with all of your heart and lean not on your understanding. Proverbs 3:5

May God bless us and renew us today!

<u>My Daily Commitment</u>

#TodayIWill do a moral and spiritual inventory of what I really treasure to make sure my heart is not vulnerable.

DAY 35

Bold Choices

God's Word

"The members of the council were amazed when they saw the boldness of Peter and John, for they could see that they were ordinary men with no special training in the Scriptures. They also recognized them as men who had been with Jesus." - Acts 4:13, NLT

How I See It

We are the accumulations of the choices we make. Every choice we make takes us closer to one thing and farther away from another. I've made some very poor choices in my life that have taken me far away from God. But I have also made some very wise choices that have brought me much closer to Him. We are the sum total of the choices we make. But one thing I have noticed is every choice I made that brought me closer to Him was a bold purposeful choice.

In college, I was a partier. I made choices that made me popular and like the "cool" people. I drank and had terrible language. While I was making those choices, they didn't seem like choices at all. They certainly were not bold. They were default and easy. And destructive. I was as far from God as a person could be.

When I graduated, I made choices for success. I was focused on money and stuff. I made choices based on what would give me more of those things. At that point in my life, I was making choices based on others expectations and cultural norms. Actually, I forfeited my power of choice to do what other people said I should do in order to achieve success and material things. I was just executing on the choices that were made for me. It is easy to just do what you are told in exchange for what you want

But one morning I made a bold choice. It was a choice to deflect blame. I chose to put whether my wife and I would have a baby or not in God's hands. What sounds like a faithful move on my part was really just creating a scapegoat for our disappointment, ineptness, and frustration. When we finally gave up trying to have a child, we could blame God rather than ourselves.

What I learned 1 month later was that it was bold to challenge God. It was bold to tell Him things are impossible. It was bold to tell Him how things are going to work. That bold choice (which resulted in our oldest son) was the beginning of a steady walk closer to Him.

Since then, I have made bold choices to attend different churches, change careers, & let people fail. Bold choices to quit something that was good to me but wasn't good for me. Bold choices to forgive people that hurt me. Every time I've made a bold choice, I get closer to God. More dependent on His provision. More reliant on His guidance. Our proximity to God is directly related to our willingness to make bold choices. May God inspire you and me to make bold choices this very week.

My Daily Commitment

#TodayIWill make a bold choice and have faith this choice will move me closer to God.

DAY 36

Soil

<u>God's Word</u>

"Listen! A farmer went out to plant some seeds. As he scattered them across his field, some seeds fell on a footpath, and the birds came and ate them. Other seeds fell on shallow soil with underlying rock. The seeds sprouted quickly because the soil was shallow. But the plants soon wilted under the hot sun, and since they didn't have deep roots, they died. Other seeds fell among thorns that grew up and choked out the tender plants. Still other seeds fell on fertile soil, and they produced a crop that was thirty, sixty, and even a hundred times as much as had been planted! Anyone with ears to hear should listen and understand." - Matthew 13: 3-9, NLT

<u>How I See It</u>

Throughout the bible, it gives many analogies of planting and growing. The story of the farmer who scatters seeds told in Matthew 13:1 focuses on the soil the seeds landed in. It tells that some fell on the path, some fell on shallow rocky soil, yet others fell among thorns, and finally some fell on good soil. Jesus makes a big deal about the soil being the key to fruitful growth.

It reminds me of a flower. If a flower doesn't bloom after a season, is our first option to pull it up and plant another one in the exact same place? Of course not. We try to figure out how we can enhance the soil to give it a better chance. We may water it more, add fertilizer, give it more sun or more shade, and then give it time to thrive in the new conditions.

The fruitfulness of our lives can be like that flower. We feel distant from God. We make unwise choices. We get tangled up in sin. Or we find ourselves just going through the motions. We all go through seasons where we are not bearing fruit. And if we want to change that, it starts with our soil.

We are where we are. While we have a choice to uproot ourselves, our best opportunity to thrive is to address the environment we are trying to grow in. God made us good. We are all made to produce fruit but we can only do that in good soil. Watering is synonymous with cleansing. We may need the cleansing that forgiveness provides. We may need to be fertilized. What more intense nutrient do we need to feed our minds, bodies, & spirits? Do we not have enough exposure to the Son? Yes, I said Son. Do we need to come out of the darkness and allow church and other Christian friends to expose us to more Son?

And finally, when we make these adjustments to the soil we are living in, we must give it time to work. While feelings of peace can come overnight, the fruit comes over a season. Be patient with yourself as you grow day by day with the enhancements you've made to your environment.

My Daily Commitment

#TodayIWill do 1 thing that makes my soil more capable of producing spiritual fruit

DAY 37

Experience Is The Best Teacher

<u>God's Word</u>

"To illustrate the point further, Jesus told them this story: "A man had two sons. The younger son told his father, 'I want my share of your estate now before you die.' So his father agreed to divide his wealth between his sons." - Luke 15:11-12, NLT

<u>How I See It</u>

In the story of the prodigal son, it is easy to read right over a powerful and timeless parenting lesson. The younger son rudely and arrogantly came to his father and wanted his inheritance now. What 99% of us would probably be thinking at that moment is "are you crazy?" and then it would move to "if you ever talk to me that way again I'll…". We would be offended and then later hurt.

But what the father in the story did was agree. I believe he knew the only way his younger son was going to grow into the man he needed to be was to experience life and the consequences of his decisions. It was obvious the young son wasn't going to listen to his father because he had a great situation there already. It was obvious he had not learned from his older brother who had modeled success by staying home and being a hard worker. So how did the dad teach his young son about life? He let him fail …

and even at the father's sacrifice of money and the father knowing it was going to hurt... both of them.

Don't you know the father knew it was a radical idea. He had to be torn between feelings of wanting his young son to learn about life but not wanting him to hurt himself. He wants to protect his son, but knows his son will run out from behind that shield any day now anyway. This was a lesson that was going to set the younger son up for life. So the father felt it was worth it.

I think parents today could learn a lot from the father. Experience is the best teacher. Not protection. Failure teaches us a whole lot more than being shielded from the consequences of our own decisions. We have to be willing to endure the pain of seeing our kids bump into life if we really want to prepare them for life beyond the nest.

Just like God allows us to fail to bring us closer to Him, we must allow the young people under our influence to fail so they learn lessons that will be necessary for them to have personal and spiritual success in life.

My Daily Commitment

#TodayIWill allow my kids/players/students/employees to fail. Not with the intent to harm, but to teach.

DAY 38

What About Me

God's Word

"The older brother was angry and wouldn't go in. His father came out and begged him, but he replied, 'All these years I've slaved for you and never once refused to do a single thing you told me to. And in all that time you never gave me even one young goat for a feast with my friends. Yet when this son of yours comes back after squandering your money on prostitutes, you celebrate by killing the fattened calf!' "His father said to him, 'Look, dear son, you have always stayed by me, and everything I have is yours. We had to celebrate this happy day. For your brother was dead and has come back to life! He was lost, but now he is found!'" - Luke 15:28-32, NLT

How I See It

In the story of the prodigal son, there are so many lessons. One is how many of us act like the older son.

The father gives BOTH sons their inheritance. Earlier in the story, the father divided his wealth between the 2 sons. When the younger son that blew all his money and was living a life of misery finally came back, the father threw a party for him. (personal note … As a father, If one of my boys went off the rails into a pit and finally came back home humble, I'd celebrate too.)

But the older son was furious. He was so upset that the younger son got a party thrown for him. His dad never threw him a party. He said he worked hard every day and didn't spend money on prostitutes. The older son would not even come in to enjoy the party or see his brother.

There are a few key points…

- The older son still had tremendous wealth. He did not lose anything. He is acting like something is being taken away from him by the father or the young son. He has totally forgotten the blessings that he has. How often do we lose sight of the mound of blessings we have when someone else get a teaspoon of grace? Let's not do that.

- The young son still has nothing. He still has a hard road ahead to rebuild trust, wealth, respect, honor. There is no sympathy for the younger brother by the older one. I wonder if the older brother would have come to the party, the younger brother may have started to tell about the time he was so hungry he wanted to eat what the pigs were eating. Or the fact that he had to work in the nasty pig pen. How lonely he was and the shame and pain he felt when he came to his senses that he had disgraced his family and his father. The older brother never experienced that depth of despair and pain. Shouldn't he feel thankful he made wise choices and stayed home? I guarantee you the party wasn't worth all the pain for the younger brother. Let's show compassion and see the whole story.

- How often do we let our petty jealousy get in the way of enjoying a blessing. Instead of showing 5 minutes of disappointment about the situation and getting over it, he just refused to go. He could have enjoyed all the benefits of the younger son coming back home. He could have eaten from the fatted calf. He could have celebrated and had fun. But nooooo, he pouted because he wasn't the center of attention. How often do we pout and miss out on all the fun & blessings just because we aren't the center of attention? Let's catch ourselves then get over ourselves. Don't let selfish pride keep us from enjoying life.

We'd do good to remember the older son on those days when we are tempted to say "what about me?"

<u>My Daily Commitment</u>

#TodayIWill remember the blessings I already have so I am not jealous of someone else

DAY 39

God's Will For Us

God's Word

"Rejoice always, pray continually, give thanks in all circumstances; for this is God's will for you in Christ Jesus." - 1 Thessalonians 5:16-18, NIV

How I See It

When we surrender our life to Christ, we desperately want to please Him. We desperately want to do His will. But we make doing His will seem complex. Our fear/reverence for God is so profound that we realize He is complex and mysterious. That naturally leads us to anticipating His will being complex. It's not. 1 Thessalonians 5:16-18 says this.

"Rejoice always, pray continually, give thanks in all circumstances; for this is God's will for you in Christ Jesus."

We should not get mixed up between Gods will & our destiny. Gods will is stated above. Out of the obedience to His will grows our destiny. Gods will for me is not a specific position of influence or place. It's an attitude. It's a posture toward Him.

Mark Batterson had a quote that has stuck with me and proven true every time I humble myself and go back to it. He said, "Don't seek opportunity. Seek God, and opportunity will seek you." I love that.

I think we could very easily say too...Don't seek influence. Seek God's will based on 1 Thessalonians 5, and influence will seek you.

<u>My Daily Commitment</u>

#TodayIWill rejoice always. Pray continuously. Give thanks in all circumstances because I know this is God's will for me.

DAY 40

Don't Take The Wide Path

<u>God's Word</u>

"Enter through the narrow gate. For wide is the gate and broad is the road that leads to destruction, and many enter through it. But small is the gate and narrow the road that leads to life, and only a few find it." - Matthew 7:13-14, NIV

<u>How I See It</u>

I was walking in the neighborhood one morning and my neighbor stopped to chat. He is a Vietnam veteran. He said one of his mentors over there, Matt who was a special forces guy, told him if he was ever lost in the jungle or the chopper went down in an unknown area, never take the trails to find your way back. That is the surest way to get captured or killed. Make your own path through the brush. It's not the easy way, but it is the best way. He said he thinks about Matt all the time.

As I finished my walk, I kept thinking about that. When we find ourselves lost or not knowing which way to go, don't take the easy route out. Easy usually looks like what everybody else is doing. Easy is to just give up. Easy is the path of least resistance.

Jesus said in Matthew 7 to look for the small road. That is the road that leads to life. To follow Jesus in this world, many times we have to make our own way. And many times it is going against the flow or society and culture.

My neighbor Grady said he never had to use that advice in SE Asia but has used it many times since he has been home.

<u>My Daily Commitment</u>

#TodayIWill not take the easy way. I will not follow the crowd through the wide gate and broad road

NOTES

[1] Hurt, Bruce. "Hebrew Definitions." *Precept Austin*, 13 Apr. 2017, www.preceptaustin.org/hebrew_definitions.

[2] Buford, Bob P. *Halftime*. Zondervan, 2016.

[3] Houdmann, S. Michael. "GotQuestions.org." *GotQuestions.org*, 30 Nov. 2018, www.gotquestions.org/. All scripture references are made from New American Standard Bible translation.

[4] Houdmann, S. Michael. "GotQuestions.org." *GotQuestions.org*, 30 Nov. 2018, www.gotquestions.org/.

[5] Medcalf, Joshua, and Jamie Gilbert. Burn Your Goals: the Counter Cultural Approach to Achieving Your Greatest Potential. Lulu Publishing Services, 2015.

[6] Adaptation From: Medcalf, Joshua, and Jamie Gilbert. Burn Your Goals: the Counter Cultural Approach to Achieving Your Greatest Potential. Lulu Publishing Services, 2015.

49701153R00126

Made in the USA
Columbia, SC
29 January 2019